Help Me
Heal

Help Me Heal

By the author of • Lisa Said No • Larissa's Song • Goodbye, Granny Dix • Lord, Why Am I Crying?

This book is for the hurting. You know who you are, and you feel terribly alone! You have tried everything, but you still hurt. You are so discouraged! You have grabbed every book at the Bible bookstore and devoured it with a heart full of hope. You might have been touched a little, but once again you felt that familiar disappointment. Nothing had really changed. People tell you the Holy Ghost is all sufficient, and that is true. Jesus is truly the answer. But you are filled with His Spirit, so why are you still hurting? There are some things nobody really wants to talk about. And these are the very things you are struggling with. Where do you go for help? Who knows about these secret, hidden hurts?

This is your book!

Lord, Help Me Heal!

Help Me Heal

Lynda Allison Doty, Ph.D.

Help Me Heal

by Lynda Allison Doty, Ph.D.

©1998 Word Aflame Press
  Hazelwood, MO 63042-2299

Cover Design by Paul Povolni

Unless otherwise indicated, all quotations of Scripture are from the King James Version. Some quotations are from New King James Version (NKJV), copyright 1979, 1980, 1982 by Thomas Nelson Inc., Publishers.

Printed in United States of America

Printed by

WORD AFLAME®PRESS
8855 DUNN ROAD
HAZELWOOD, MO 63042-2299

Library of Congress Cataloging-in-Publication Data

Doty, Lynda Allison.
     Help me heal / Lynda Allison Doty.
          p.   cm.
     Includes bibliographical references.
     ISBN 1-56722-213-7
     1. Suffering—Religious aspects—Christianity.   2. Spiritual healing.
Consolation.   I. Title.
BV4909.D67   1998
248.8'6—dc21   98-17613
                                                       CIP

Contents

Help Me Heal*

God, You said we could not bear our burdens on our own.
But, Lord, there are times I feel I'm doing everything
   alone.
You've given me a reason to live for every day,
And, Lord, I come before You with this one wish, I pray.

> Help me heal!
> Take away my doubts and fears;
> Help me feel Your hand wipe away my tears.
> Give me strength to carry on
> Each night and day.
> Help me heal, O Lord, I pray.

I don't ask for anything but what You can give me,
And I won't hold a thing from You; I'll give it willingly.
So many times I've wandered from the things You'd have
   me do;
So here I am, take all of me, I give my life to You.

> Help me heal!
> Take away my doubts and fears;
> Help me feel Your hand wipe away my tears.
> Give me strength to carry on
> Each night and day.
> Help me heal, O Lord, I pray.

I know it won't be easy,
But Your promises are true.
If I keep my head up high and never doubt,
I know You'll see me through!

Help me heal!
Take away my doubts and fears;
Help me feel Your hand wipe away my tears.
Give me strength to carry on
Each night and day.
Help me heal, O Lord, I pray.

*Words and music by Erica Gabler. From *Be Somebody*, a tape produced by Tupelo Children's Mansion, Tupelo, Mississippi. Used by permission.

Foreword

> *A certain man went down from Jerusalem to Jericho, and fell among thieves, which stripped him of his raiment, and wounded him, and departed, leaving him half dead. And by chance there came down a certain priest that way: and when he saw him, he passed by on the other side. And likewise a Levite, when he was at the place, came and looked on him, and passed by on the other side. But a certain Samaritan, as he journeyed, came where he was; and when he saw him, he had compassion on him, and went to him, and bound up his wounds, pouring in oil and wine, and set him on his own beast, and brought him to an inn, and took care of him. And on the morrow when he departed, he took out two pence, and gave them to the host, and said unto him, Take care of him; and whatsoever thou spendest more, when I come again, I will repay thee. Which now of these three, thinkest thou, was neighbour unto him that fell among the thieves? And he said, He that shewed mercy on him. Then said Jesus unto him, Go, and do thou likewise (Luke 10:30-37).*

The Scripture directly mandates us to help those who are hurting. When Jesus used the example of the good Samaritan, He left an indelible and directional mandate for us to help those who have been wounded along the highway of life. *"Go, and do thou likewise."*

In over twenty-five years of working with children who have been wounded through abuse, neglect, abandonment, and lack of natural love, I have learned the necessity of leaning on the Lord. I have learned to rely upon the Word . . . prayer . . . and the gifts of the word of knowledge and the word of wisdom to minister to those who are hurting.

In this simple parable, Jesus Christ teaches the secret to contentment: When we have picked people up from the roadside and applied the Holy Spirit to their wounds . . . when we have given them a place to sleep, to rest, and to heal . . . we find contentment and peace in our soul. We find sleep sweet and deep, because we have obeyed the Word of God.

When we are trying to help someone, and we have tried everything and have no place else to go, let us remember to plead the blood of Jesus—not necessarily the blood that flowed from His side, His hands, His feet, and His head, but the internal bleeding . . . the bruises . . . the blood that burst out under the skin but did not leave His broken body. This is the blood that covers and heals the hidden, emotional wounds and hurts that are down inside.

Thank God for the blood! Thank God for healing! Thank God for His mercies! We can find peace, rest, and hope in our Savior Jesus Christ.

This book adds another dimension to the multifaceted talents of Sister Lynda Allison Doty. You will be blessed as you read this book, and encouraged to reach out and help others. *"Go, and do thou likewise."*

Stephen M. Drury, President
Tupelo Children's Mansion

Preface

First Things First

I hope you will notice that I have a new name! On May 24, 1997, Lynda Allison obtained the "Mrs." degree—so I am now Lynda Allison Doty. God was so good to me! He brought me a wonderful husband. And I couldn't find one anywhere who is kinder, more understanding—or more *patient*. This book would not have been possible without him. It pays to wait on God.

It also took my experiences in New Orleans and at Tupelo Children's Mansion to make this book what it is. I am deeply grateful to Brothers John Cupit and Stephen Drury for the burden and the load that they carry. I am much better off for having worked with these men of God and very thankful to know them both.

I am indebted also to Reverend and Mrs. Kenneth Doyle for all their encouragement, love, and faith in me and to Sister Sarah Varnum for her faithful reading of manuscripts. Those who love and inspire me are too many to name, and so I will stop at this point. God bless you all; you know who you are.

"He sent his word, and healed them" (Psalm 107:20).

How Not to Use This Book

This book is written not so much to impart intellectual understanding as to minister. It is not written for the head, but for the heart.

When I first set out to get this book on paper, I planned neat little chapters with neat little titles. Adultery would have its chapter. Abuse would have its own chapter. Rape and Abortion all would be discussed in their proper places. But that plan simply did not work. It was too neat, too simplistic.

As you pick up this book, please do not glance down the table of contents and flip over to the section that seems to apply to your situation. Please do not jump around. If you do, you are going to miss too much. The keys to healing are spread throughout the entire book; they are not found in one place. I tried to make it simpler for you, I really did. But I had to write according to the timing and anointing of the Holy Spirit, and God does not always proceed according to my timetable.

How to Use This Book

I ran into a dilemma when I cited certain references. Rather than bog down the reader with footnotes, I decided just to put the name of the author plus the date in parentheses right in the text, like this: (Doty, 1998). Readers who might be interested can then go to the bibliography in the back of the book.

Now that all the housekeeping is out of the way, the first thing to do is to get your Bible. You will need it as you go through this book. It would also be helpful to have some kind of notebook handy in which to jot things down. We will be starting our journey together by taking a look at our perception . . . perspective . . . attitude. In the Word of God rests all the answers, the examples, the help we need. So read this book with your Bible in hand. It is the Word of God that brings change, not the pages of this book or any other book.

As we study together to determine just where our attitudes lie, you may find that they do not line up with the Word of God. And you may discover further, that you are not in a place yet emotionally where you can *make* them line up. Now this is a tricky place to be, because you will be tempted to get discouraged. But rejoice instead—because this is simply telling you that more healing is needed—and God is standing ready. For *you*!

As you read this book . . . and as you bask in God's healing balm throughout its pages . . . you will discover a gradual shifting of your priorities and perceptions. When you begin to notice this, you will experience a quickening down deep inside. That is the Holy Ghost telling you, *Yes, child, I am working!*

When this begins to happen, rejoice. Sure, it will be gradual, barely perceptible in places. But I am asking you to thank and praise God for every little change, every little way He is working with you and in you. "In all thy ways acknowledge him, and he shall direct thy paths" (Proverbs 3:6). Acknowledge Him by praise and thanksgiving in the small things, big things, bad things. I promise—this works.

Take your Bible out now and keep it with you as you work your way through this book. You will be asked to study many verses of Scripture with me. Look up the verses of Scripture; do not take my word for them. Read them and allow them to minister to you. That is where your help lies. Be willing to get into the Word.

Isaiah 10:27 tells us that the yoke shall be destroyed because of the anointing. The pages of this book can become a point of contact for you—something in the physical realm that can unleash faith in the supernatural realm. There is no magic in these pages. But as you open yourself to the ministry of the Holy Spirit, anointing can flow from God to you through this channel. The yoke is destroyed because of the anointing. The anointing brings healing.

I once counseled a young woman who was very intent on getting healed. Her loved ones had just about given up on her and had lost all patience with her. When I work with a person, I always assign homework and that includes much Scripture. One day she called me up and asked, "Do I really have to read *all* these verses of Scripture?"

"Read them all." I replied.

"But I mean, I've read them over and over so much I know what they're going to say."

"Great. But read them all. It's like filling a glass of water under a faucet. Soon it will overflow with clean, clear water. That is where you will find your healing. Jesus told His disciples in John 15:3, 'Ye are clean through the word.'"

She obeyed and was healed, all because of the Word of God and the Spirit ministering the Word to her and in her. The sparkle returned to her eyes, and she has resumed her rightful place in society. She is fully functioning, because of *Him.*

Just *handling* the Bible can edify!

It is my prayer that this book will lead you into a life-changing experience—either for you, or for someone you care about, . . . or maybe both.

Chapter 1

⁓

Introduction

*"When my father and my mother forsake me,
then the* LORD *will take me up" (Psalm 27:10).*

"The tiny little newborn lay in its crib, tired, hungry, wet, soiled. It cried and cried, and no one came. Its little wet face scrunched up, and the tiny fingers flailed the air. Finally, its little head rolled over, its cheek touching the soiled sheet of the crib. With a heavy sigh, old beyond her mere days, she gave up. It did no good to cry. No use to wait. No use to hurt. No one would come. No one would help.

"The room was dark and cold. The fire in the kerosene stove in the corner had gone out long ago. The pungent odor of kerosene lingered in the air, burning the tiny nostrils, making the little stomach queasy. A drawn window shade let in a tiny slither of light.

"The little one had learned so soon that no one cared. Except, there had been one person, a beautiful young lady, who came just about the same time every afternoon. From the way the girl talked to her, the baby thought this might be her older sister, home from school. The first place the older sister went was into this little nursery. And each day she found the same sight. The newborn cold, wet, soiled, hungry—and finally no longer able or willing to cry out. At last, the little newborn quit fighting; she just gave up."

This book is written for the person who is hurting. You know who you are. You know you need healing, but you have tried everything and you still need healing. Your situation is discouraging. You have gone to counselors, from therapy to therapy perhaps. You have grabbed every book in your local Bible bookstore, taken it home, and devoured it with a heart full of hope. You might have been touched a little, but for the most part you once again felt that familiar disappointment. Nothing has really changed.

There are some things nobody really wants to talk about. And these are the very things you are struggling with. Where do you go for help? So many in the church feel helpless to assist you. They just do not have the expertise and understanding that you need. And sometimes, when you venture to mention these kinds of things, they look so shocked that you just back off. Then there are worldly counselors trained in these specific areas, but you do not really want to go to them. So you just do not know where to turn.

One hurting sister told me, "I don't know how much longer I can take this. I have been in such intense pain for years. A lot of people have tried to help me, but they've given up. When I come around now, they turn away. It's not that they don't care, I'm sure; it's just that they don't know what else to do with me."

Another lady in the counseling room said, "I was dying spiritually. I was faithful to church, I did everything the preacher told me to do, but I was dying. I finally gave up and just started crying out to God, every day, every day, 'Jesus! Help me heal! I don't know what's wrong with me, just *help me heal!*'"

This book is not a piece of magic, and nothing is going to be done merely through my words. But this book is written for *you*, in answer to your prayer, and will accomplish what He wants it to accomplish. "So shall my word be that goeth forth out of my mouth: it shall not return unto me void, but it shall accomplish that which I please, and it shall prosper in the thing whereto I sent it" (Isaiah 55:11). "He sent his word, and healed them" (Psalm 107:20).

It is also written for the person who longs to help the hurting person. Perhaps you have been likewise hurt and healed and cannot understand why other people are still stuck in the hurting mode. Or perhaps you have never been through anything like this and do not understand, even though you want to help. This question comes from a letter I received from a pastor's wife: "Lynda, can you help me with a young woman I'm working with? I don't know what it's like not to be wanted by my parents. Both my parents loved me and wanted me. I can love this girl, but I just can't understand! What can I say to her that will help?"

And here is part of a telephone conversation: "I was raised in this truth; I used to sleep beneath the pews. I've never known anything else. I'm having such a hard time relating to what these people are telling me!"

A pastor confided: "I can preach the gospel and lay hands on the sick. I can do a lot of things. But I just don't know how to deal with a rape victim or a woman who has killed her own baby by abortion. It's not that I condemn them—I just don't know what to say."

I just don't know how to deal with a rape victim or a woman who has killed her own baby by abortion.

Another pastor: "I have an almost impossible time dealing with the women [in my church]. I can't counsel alone with them and yet their problems are intensely personal. Could you come here for a few days and work with them?"

Here is e-mail from a pastor's wife: "I guess I lived a very sheltered life. When I try to talk with these people, I draw a blank. I just can't understand. I'm afraid I might be doing them more harm than good."

This is a book that, I hope, can answer some of the questions. The need to write it really began to burn with intensity while I was at Tupelo Children's Mansion. There my heart was broken by so many things that I saw. Still I resisted writing this book, because I knew that in doing so I would have to deal with some hurts in my own life that I had buried long ago. I wanted to do the book, but I knew I could not write a book for the hurting without experiencing the hurt. What I write about has to come from deep within my own spirit.

Like you, I do not want to hurt. Most of us, as a part of humankind, will choose to deny our pain until it gets so bad that we know we have to do something—anything— to stop the pain. The bulk of the people I work with are in that category. Their pain has become so bad that they are willing to work. They are willing to obey the Word of God to find healing.

Some clients have requested that I help them remember their past, to bring back hidden memories that they feel they need to be healed of. I consistently refuse. I do not believe in using techniques of regression and hypnosis to cause so-called memories of the past to surface. I believe this process should be left up to God, if and when He sees that we are ready. God brings our memories to light in His own time, and He reveals them to us for a purpose—not so that we can feel sorry for our lot in life but so we can overcome them, through Him!

My husband tells about a particular hurt in his background, a trauma that involved his whole family. He pushed it aside, "forgot" about it, and went on with his life. For years he lived without thinking of that trauma. But the night came when, after attempting so many times to receive the Holy Ghost, he asked God, "What's wrong, Lord? Why can't I receive the Holy Ghost?" And that was when the Lord brought the trauma back to his mind. My husband needed to forgive the person who had caused all the pain. Instantly, he began to forgive him, and just as instantly, God filled my husband with the Holy Spirit! But it was God's timing, not man's.

God is able to provide what we need, and He wants to do it. He does not want us to remain crippled in this lifetime. As we study the accounts in the Bible, we find lame and blind people who were not healed until a certain time—because God had a plan! And it was to bring Him glory!

The memory at the beginning of this chapter of the newborn infant is one such memory that the Lord caused to surface. That little one was me. I was not seeking memories; it was triggered by a scene from my past. It had been many years since I had visited the place of my birth in South Carolina. God's presence accompanied me as I drove through the streets. His presence was strong, and tears flowed freely. I recalled past Christmases, past holidays. My grandfather's death. Walks with my sister in downtown Florence. Shopping at the dime store. Playing on the wide front porch. Swinging on the tire in the yard. These were bittersweet memories.

At first I felt anger bordering on rage. How could anyone allow an innocent baby to suffer so!

I was not seeking any particular memories. But then the infant memory came. At first I felt anger bordering on rage. How could anyone allow an innocent baby to suffer so! Who had such a right!

Next came the hurt, as the realization sank in that the little one was *me*. Deep hurt, sorrow that I had even been born. I must say, though, in fairness to my parents, they were not aware of what was going on. My dad was off earning a living and my mother was ill and bedfast. As far as they knew, I was being cared for. They did not know that my caretaker was too busy doing *other* things.

The fact is, in today's terminology, this family was dysfunctional. It is probable that, had abortions been encouraged then as now, more than likely I would have been aborted. I arrived very late in my parents' lives, and a new baby created a true hardship. But the timing of my birth and the family into which I was born, were, I believe with my whole heart, ordained by God. He knew me before I was even formed in the womb. And then He used everything that happened to me throughout my life to mold me into the person He wanted me to be, for the work He had planned for me.

He could have chosen another family for me to be born into. He told Jeremiah, "Before thou was formed in the womb I knew thee." But God placed me into this particular family. And if God is omniscient, all knowing—if He indeed knows the beginning and the end—then He knew these things would happen to me. Beyond that I cannot understand, but this I know: When my father and my mother forsook me, the Lord Himself took me up.

Why does revival not come to many churches? Sometimes it may be because we have so many wounded in our churches already. What would the wounded do with all the new babies? If we are not whole, we are not yet who we should be in God. He has work and assignments for us that we are not fully capable of performing yet. We must become emotionally and spiritually whole. Why? Because we have got to be able to minister to others. Sister Dorian, a friend in Louisiana, hit the nail on the head: "God led me to a group where I realized that suppressed, hidden feelings, emotional wounds and scars prohibited me from being all that God created me to be and that the pain was actually the struggle within to be the person God designed."

When we hurt, we focus on self. We have to get self out of the way. Revival does not come to a church filled with self. When we focus on God, not on self, we will have revival. No doubt, that is why many poverty-stricken countries are having great revival. The people have nothing to turn to except God, and they focus on Him.

Tough Issues

What will we do with the new breed of converts praying through at our altars? They have different kinds of problems: divorce, rape, incest, drugs, abortion, prodigal children in prison, child abuse. . . . We will deal with these issues individually as we go through this book. What about you? If a homosexual sits down beside you in church, what do you do? How do you minister to this kind of person? What about the drug addict whose smell nauseates you?

If a homosexual sits down beside you in church, what do you do? How do you minister to this kind of person?

But to compound the problem, troubles in these last days are not limited to the new converts and the bizarre things they can bring from the world. Third- and fourth-generation Pentecostals are also suffering at Satan's merciless hand. The widow of a minister sat quietly in the congregation week after week, smiling, praying for others, being a blessing to everyone. One day she told me, "I just feel like quitting. I can't stand the pain anymore." I learned that she had been abused by her minister-husband and that this nightmare was still a part of her existence.

What about the woman who had seven abortions before coming to the Lord? Do we tell her that her past is under the blood and to go and sin no more? It is true that her past is under the blood. But when Jesus told people to go and sin no more, it was after He had touched them. Women who have killed their own offspring must come face to face with that fact, and something has to be done with the wounds. Jesus must touch them. He must heal them.

"When my father and my mother forsake me, then the Lord will take me up." These are the kinds of children who come to Tupelo Children's Mansion. Kids who have been forsaken and the Lord has taken up. Children who are bruised and wounded. I so much appreciate the work they are doing there with the children. The staff are sensitive people, drawn to the Mansion because they care. People who care have tender hearts that break easily. I have cried with staff members overwhelmed by the needs.

Life at the Mansion is a life of work. Having lived there, I know that the children's needs always come first. The staff runs short of time; there is so much to be done. So much to do, so little time, so little help. They are doing a good work for God. One such "work" was Erica Gabler, the young lady who penned the words and music to the beautiful song by the same name as this book.

Erica's Story

Erica has hurt most of her young life. She told me recently that her grandfather just died, and she was hurting right then about that. But even through the tears, she told me, "God can do it."

When I first mentioned to Erica about writing something for this book, she was thrilled to learn that her song had touched the lives of so many. "I just had no idea my song touched you," she told me.

"That's the neat thing about serving God," I said. "Our lives touch people we will never know. At least, not in this lifetime."

"I did get a few letters about the song," she said.

Erica was so surprised and so pleased to learn that she had had a part in touching people's lives. "I struggled, all my life, with rejection," Erica said. "Rejection from the time I was a little kid. Things hurt so much then, and I guess I carried them with me all my life.

"When I wrote 'Help Me Heal,' I had been going through a whole lot. I just didn't feel I could go on any more. I'd kinda reached the end, you know? I decided to write a letter to God. I sat down with pen and paper and at the top of the page I wrote, 'Dear God.' I felt so helpless, so empty.

"And I began to write Him a letter, telling Him how I felt, pouring out my hurts to Him. I didn't know what else to do! And as I wrote, it began to dawn on me that some of the words were beginning to rhyme. So then I began to see that it looked like some kind of song was taking shape. So then I wrote the chorus and then the second verse and the bridge. And God had helped me write a whole song!

"I never could have done it without the Mansion," Erica went on. "I would never be where I am today without the Mansion. They've helped me so much. They got counseling for me. They were always there for me, you know what I mean? Anytime I needed somebody, there was somebody there for me. If I needed to talk, there was somebody willing to listen."

I can still see Erica on the platform singing that song. My heart was so touched by this child singing to her God. I knew she had been through so much. All the kids who come to the Mansion have been through more than a child should have to go through. I asked Erica what, if anything, she would tell the people reading this book . . .

what would she tell the person who was hurting and who, like Erica, felt she could not go on. Erica said to tell them, "Turn it over to God. Let Him take care of it."

That sounds so simple, but Erica knows it is not as simple as it sounds. But each of us can do it. Erica did. And God will do it. He did it for Erica. So this is a book about pain, about the hurts that are still not healed. Perhaps we can say the whole book is about how to turn everything over to God. He is surely the answer. He surely holds the key.

Chapter 2

~

Beyond the Tears

"And a certain man lame from his mother's womb . . ." (Acts 3:2).

The man at Gate Beautiful in Acts 3 was lame from his mother's womb. As a result of his wonderful healing, we go on to read in Acts 4:4 that about five thousand souls were saved. If we can learn to look at our own "handicaps" in this way, we will be in a position to be greatly used by God. And isn't that what we want more than anything?

This pitiful lame man was reduced to being a beggar. We can imagine his childhood, how he must have been laughed at and made fun of. The Bible does not tell us, but we can imagine how much pain he endured. If only he could have looked ahead into the future and seen in a vision or a dream—or only by faith—what plans the Lord had for him!

Let us pray for God to give us such a vision. Once we learn to focus on God's plan for our lives, we will see everything differently and things will begin to change. Our circumstances will take on new meaning. Instead of begging God to get us out of our circumstances, we will ask for grace to get through them, holding onto His dear hand.

Let us listen to these words from the depths of an aching heart:

"The trauma of being victimized by incest stole reality from me. It was as if my whole world had been rearranged in less than ten minutes' time. I began living in and reacting to a world that seemed very real to me. However, this world and my new belief system were so far from being true that my behavior began to perplex everyone around me. Those close to me were left wondering what was wrong with this little girl who had so recently played, laughed, and reacted as a typical ten-year-old child. Why had she changed?"

These words were written by a friend. This was the result of only one event of sexual abuse on her young body. Years later, after much more senseless pain, she would go on to become institutionalized in a mental hospital and make several serious suicide attempts.

What pain, what tears I feel in her words and have seen in her life. How difficult it must have been for her, in a mental institution, to see beyond the tears. Like Joseph of old, sold as a slave and imprisoned for doing well—how difficult it is to see beyond the tears.

Let us never get caught up with licking our wounds from the past. If we hurt, let us go to our knees and take our tears to God. If it is time to recall long-forgotten memories, He will allow them to surface. When it is time to be healed, our Lord and Savior Jesus Christ will bring it to pass.

A fellow student in my eighth grade class had a very large head and walked with a limp. Most of the kids made fun of him—some openly, right to his face. This boy did not have a coat, and it was an icy, bone-chilling winter. I begged my mother to buy him a coat. Her heart went out to him, and together we shopped for a beautiful red wool jacket. I felt that red would perk him up.

I went to his locker and sneaked the jacket inside. I

lurked close by, dizzy with excitement, wanting him to hurry up and find his jacket. I will never forget the look on his face when he did. First, he looked puzzled. Then he looked around him, as though worried if this could be yet another brutal joke. His eyes moved up and down the hallway, empty except for me, pretending to be fiddling in my own locker. And then his hands began to stroke the red wool, and he looked longingly at the garment. Finally, he tried it on. And the look of joy and wonderment warmed my heart beyond words. That was a powerful lesson on giving! I don't know that he grew up to be healed, as in Acts 3. But I thank God for giving me the privilege of contributing something good to this boy's life. God used this boy to minister to me, although he never knew about it.

God can take our hurts and use them in a great way to accomplish His purpose. I have seen it—I have experienced it—time and time again! God has a plan and a purpose for each of us, and He is the one who decides how to use us. Even before time began for us—before we came to rest in our mother's womb—God loved us, and God had a plan and a purpose for us. He does not cause someone to be created just to vegetate through this life.

He makes the blind and the lame. Even those people we look at and pity, the ones who are retarded and malformed—God has a purpose for them. Many times, He uses them to reveal Himself through healing. When God called Moses to speak His message to Pharaoh and Moses gave the excuse that he was not an eloquent speaker, God answered, "Who has made man's mouth? Or who makes the mute, the deaf, the seeing, or the blind? Have not I, the LORD?" (Exodus 4:11, NKJV). In other words, God is in control of everyone, and He can use each one of us, despite our limitations or handicaps, for His glory.

27

The Blind Man

And as Jesus passed by, he saw a man which was blind from his birth. And his disciples asked him, saying, Master, who did sin, this man, or his parents, that he was born blind? Jesus answered, Neither hath this man sinned, nor his parents: but that the works of God should be made manifest in him (John 9:1-3).

A few verses later this man washed in the pool of Siloam at the command of Jesus, and he was healed. A great controversy erupted because Jesus healed the man on the Sabbath, and the Pharisees tried to get the healed man to denounce Jesus as a sinner. The man responded with some of the most beautiful words in the Bible: "Whether he be a sinner or no, I know not: one thing I know, that, whereas I was blind, now I see" (John 9:25).

After more disputation, the healed man met Jesus again, and upon learning that Jesus was the Son of God, he worshiped Him. Jesus explained, "For judgment I am come into this world, that they which see not might see; and that they which see might be made blind" (John 9:39).

Everyone has a purpose in the plan of God, even those who are blind or lame or unable to speak properly.

From this story, we see that everyone has a purpose in the plan of God, even those who are blind or lame or unable to speak properly.

Therefore, we ought to rejoice even in suffering, knowing that God has a plan to use us for His glory. Paul instructed, "Rejoice in the Lord alway: and again I say, Rejoice" (Philippians 4:4). It is not easy to rejoice when we are in the midst of suffering. But if we do choose to rejoice, the quality of the suffering changes. It becomes lighter, more poignant, perhaps. It becomes spiritual! Peter explained, "If, when ye do well, and suffer for it, ye take it patiently, this is acceptable with God. For even hereunto were ye called: because Christ also suffered for us, leaving us an example, that ye should follow his steps. . . . But and if ye suffer for righteousness' sake, happy are ye" (I Peter 2:20-21; 3:14).

Peter did not say "If ye suffer because ye are righteous." He said, "If ye suffer *for righteousness' sake.*" There is a difference; he spoke from the perspective of motive. For example, if my next-door neighbor parks in my driveway and I do not say anything to him, I am simply allowing him to park in my driveway. But suppose he asks me if he can park there, because workers will be utilizing his driveway that day. Although it will inconvenience me slightly and I would really rather he didn't, I grant him this permission. I do it for his sake. The dictionary defines "sake" as "purpose; motive; someone else's advantage; or good; their personal benefit or interest; welfare." In other words the purpose behind the act is what counts. It is of no benefit to suffer just to be suffering. But if we suffer for the sake of righteousness, then our suffering is not in vain.

Our suffering has meaning, then, when we totally, absolutely abandon ourselves to God and His purpose. Then He is in His rightful place: first in our lives, on the throne of our hearts. That is where He must sit. When we have Him there, we become so lost in Him, so sold out to Him, that we are at last able to obey His command to love our enemies and those who persecute us. We thus see how important it is, not necessarily to work on being healed of our past pain, but to seek the face of God and His fullness. Then everything else—purpose, meaning, healing—can follow.

Suffering is like going down a flight of stairs. Each

step we take down is into a deeper experience with God. If we can learn to look upon our circumstances in this way, our lives will be transformed. Instead of having a panic attack, we will remain calm. Instead of being consumed with fear, we will develop a strong inner courage.

They that wait upon the LORD shall renew their strength (Isaiah 40:31).

There is one thing needful in this life and that is to rest at the feet of Jesus. Why, then, do we find it so hard to do? We are so rushed, so busy doing His work, that resting in His presence often seems—well, for lack of a better word, wasteful. After all, we need to hurry up and ask Him for what we need so we can go about His business. We check in, and just as soon as we have touched Him, we dart out, thinking we have accomplished something because we have touched Him. But touching Jesus is only the beginning! Once we have touched Him, then we have actually entered into the realm of prayer. We have His undivided attention. Now is the time to begin real prayer. Oh, how impatient we are!

It reminds me of this imaginary scene: a beloved friend I would really like to visit with comes to my door. As soon as I answer and fling wide the door, she says, "Just dropped by to say hi. Gotta run. See ya later."

"Wait! Wait!" my heart cries out with disappointment. I am left alone with thoughts of sharing secrets over coffee. There's an emptiness tinged with frustration.

I wonder if that is how the Lord feels. Does He feel a certain loneliness for us when we leave our prayer closet too soon? Do His eyes follow wistfully after us, hoping we will come back and stay awhile?

"Lord, Heal My Hurt"
Sister Dorian is a wonderful lady who serves God with

a big heart. It was not always that way for Dorian. She had to come through the tears first. Here is her testimony:

"For years I was engulfed with pain so intense that it often took my breath away. It was a hurt that I could not put into words, yet it was undeniable. It prohibited my growth in God, and I knew that temporary relief would not be the solution. I needed to be healed, but the scary part was that I did not know the source of the pain. I did know that if I did not receive a healing for the mysterious pain that I would die spiritually and probably physically, too. So, constantly and continuously I prayed, 'Lord, heal my hurt.' Finally after many sleepless nights and much crying, the Lord said, 'That's enough! This is the answer.'

I needed to be healed, but the scary part was that I did not know the source of the pain.

"He led me to a group where I realized that suppressed and hidden feelings, emotional wounds and scars prohibited me from being all that God created me to be and that the pain was actually the struggle within to be the person God designed.

"God healed me and I became a new creature in Christ Jesus. Now, all of this did not happen overnight. Nevertheless, I can tell you that God is a perfect gentleman; He did not heal any area of my life that I was not willing to allow Him to enter into."

"I Have Seen Thy Tears" (Isaiah 38:5)

Baby woke with a howl. One could tell by his cry that he had a real need. His young mother rushed to his rescue and lifted her baby into her arms. The terrible noise subsided somewhat, but a big, fat tear rolled from the corner of his eye and down his cheek.

"Poor baby," I said, as another tear fell. His eyes gazed into mine with his unspoken request, his little lips quivering.

His mother wiped his tears away and began to nurse her hungry little son. "Doesn't it break your heart," she said, "to see a baby's tears like that?"

How true, I thought. Babies cry and babies fuss, and we adults snap to attention, but there is just something about those tears that really touch our hearts. We would go to the ends of the earth for such a helpless, needy infant.

As I sat there watching mother and son, I thought about how much our tears must touch God's heart. After all, He is our Father, and we are His children. He cares! When our hearts are heavy and we are empty and lonely, we can be sure that our heavenly Father takes notice of our tears. It breaks His heart to see our tears. It is wonderful to have such a loving, caring God!

God is the best psychiatrist available!

We thank You, Lord, for Your love and understandingand for the gift of tears. After the tears comes peace. After the tears . . . joy. After the tears . . . grace.

Chapter 3

~

The Effects of Pain

One morning I received a telephone call from a minister who wanted to thank me for my book *Lord, Why Am I Crying?* She told me that a real prayer warrior in her church, who had been struggling and suffering for years, had made a complete turnaround after reading the book. She said that the woman was like a different person. Naturally, I rejoiced to hear this news.

She went on to explain that this woman had been abused emotionally by her mother. She had been hurt so badly that as an adult she could not trust anyone. She would allow herself to start getting close to other saints in the church, then she would withdraw, leaving the others frustrated, wondering what on earth they had done wrong this time.

How do people like this pull away and withdraw? Usually by becoming obnoxious, hard to put up with. Or they just disappear off the scene for a while.

Judy was like that, always disappearing. Just as we would make some progress, off she would run. I would not hear from her for a long time. Then suddenly, out of the blue, here would come a phone call. "Lynda! This is Judy!" We would catch up on the news, and she would promise that *this* time she was going to stay put, for sure. *This* time, it would be different!

But, you guessed it, she would eventually disappear again.

These hurting people excel at making excuses. No matter what solution someone suggests to them, it will not work. Or, it has already been tried and has failed. It is too complicated, or it is too simple. I call this attitude the "Yes, but" syndrome.

This attitude makes it hard for concerned workers to help these people. Friends are left feeling stranded and adrift, not knowing what to do next. It can be frustrating when time after time we are stabbed in the back by someone we are trying to help.

What is going on with a person like that? Let us listen to these words from the depths of Judy's heart:

"All my life I was punished, even when I didn't do anything wrong. I soon decided that maybe I was just making it up when I thought I had done nothing wrong. The people who loved me ought to know. And they punished me. So my child brain just began to assume I was always wrong.

"When I grew up and some things started going right for me, I couldn't accept them. And so I would do something to sabotage it. Like my marriage. Like getting really close in counseling, close to a breakthrough. Then I'd hurt you, jab at you, anything to make you leave me alone. When that wouldn't work, I'd split. Leave the state. Can you understand what I'm saying?"

People are crying out for help. They yearn for us to pull some kind of "magic" out of the proverbial hat and make the pain go away.

Actually, people like this are crying out for help. They yearn for us to pull some kind of "magic" out of the proverbial hat and make the pain go away.

But they are so afraid of being hurt again that they just give up. They are not aware of what they are doing. Their behavior is an example of the effects of pain on the human personality.

The effects of being hurt can last a lifetime. Some of the things I went through as a child, I have come to realize were inflicted on me because the adults in my life had also been wounded as children, and they had never discovered the tools to overcome it. The abused often becomes the abuser! But we, the people of the name of Jesus, have the tools! And when it is time to be healed, our Lord and Savior Jesus Christ will bring it to pass.

"All Fear Is Gone"

I have known and loved Sandy for a long time. When she heard I was writing this book, she told me I simply *had* to write about fear. She told me how abuse had paralyzed her for years—through fear. "All pain," she said, "pain of any kind, causes fear. The abused person is afraid to go through abuse again. Afraid it will happen all over again. Afraid to suffer!"

My heart used to break as I watched her suffer over and over from things in her past. She was doing a fantastic work for God. She loved God with her whole mind and soul and being. If I had ever seen anyone I could call a real Christian, it was Sandy. And yet she was still crying inside from hurts from yesteryear.

I recently talked with her again and was absolutely thrilled with her good report:

"God heals us little by little, and sometimes we don't even know it's happening. We aren't even aware that He's working. About a year ago, an evangelist came to our church. At the altar service we started singing, 'Because He Lives.' I'd never been able to sing that particular song since my husband died. Now I was singing it, but I was numb. When we got to the words 'all fear is gone' I stopped mouthing the words. I realized suddenly that I couldn't sing that, because of all the fear I had!

"I started thinking, Here I am forty-eight years old. I'm supposed to have been a Christian for so long, and I don't even know how to trust God! Here I am, so scared. I don't know how to trust God. I just broke. . . ."

Sandy continued, "That was in September. In December I went home for the holidays. At the church there, too, the people started singing the same song. Isn't that just like God? When He's dealing with us about something, He just won't let up. So they were singing that song there in my daughter's church. Without really thinking about it, I was singing along, 'All fear is gone.' Suddenly the Lord snapped His fingers in my ears, and I realized I had sung those words! I had actually sung those words!

"Then later, in Georgia, at yet another church—you guessed it—they started singing the same song. And I sang, and I realized that—somehow, somewhere—God had delivered me. When they asked me for a testimony, I stood and told what God had done, that He had delivered me from fear.

"After the service a lady came to me sobbing. She said no one knew how she had been struggling with fear and how desperately she had needed to hear my testimony. That's what it's all about, sister. Being healed so we can help others!"

Something Sandy said really hit home: pain of any kind causes fear. It seems God's people are being gripped by fear more and more. The worse the world becomes, the more God's people are being affected by fear. This should not be! And yet I understand it.

I remember one lady who was robbed in the parking lot of a church. It happened in broad daylight on a sunny Sunday morning. After that, some people started coming to church less and less. They were afraid it might happen to them. They were gripped, paralyzed by fear. What a powerful tool the enemy has at his disposal!

Over and over I hear of people who refuse to act

because of fear. Some will not drive in the fog or the rain or the dark because of fear. Some cannot sleep, will not witness, will not knock on a door. Some people in New Orleans do not leave their homes during the entire time of Mardi Gras because of fear. To my surprise, believers have told me they are on medication for panic attacks. They are afraid to go out, afraid to come in, afraid to answer the door, afraid to go to a fellowship meeting on the other side of town. This world is an evil place and grows more so every day. We must exercise wisdom. But I also know the Word of God says that He has not given us a spirit of fear. "Fear not!" says our Lord. "Trust in Me! Lean not unto your own understanding!"

How a Child Learns

A little girl grows up sexually abused, finally marries, and goes on to live happily ever after. However, the wedding night brings unwanted surprises, and memories snap back, memories too painful to handle. She begins to develop physical symptoms. Migraine headaches, for example, can keep her husband at bay. She is not aware of it. He is not aware of it. But it is an example of the effects of pain on our personality.

Husbands in this situation can play such a critical role, if they will only be loving and patient. One husband I know pushed right past my client's pain and fear, insisting that his own selfish needs be met. If he only could have realized how much damage he was causing!

When a child receives hurt from the hand of someone who is appointed to protect and nurture her, that child experiences the effects of this for a lifetime. But the gift of the Holy Ghost can lead her to complete healing. She can learn new ways of behaving and, yes, even new ways of feeling.

A little girl, for example, who is abused by her father, will grow up to have a distorted view of what a father really is. If her father molested her, beat her physically, neglected her, or abused her with ugly words that hurt, she will find it difficult to relate to a heavenly Father who is all good and nurturing. She will tend to see God the same way her dad was.

I was never abused by my father, but I did learn from him early on that fathers can be very ineffective. If I appealed to him, mother would interfere and overrule. I learned that my father did not have any clout. It did no good to go to him. He might sympathize with me, and he truly wanted the best for me, and for that I am thankful. But as far as actually causing any change in my life and circumstances, he did not. Therefore, it has been a struggle for me to accept—at heart level—that my heavenly Father has all power in heaven and earth and can answer any prayer that I pray.

An Introverted Personality

Many times abused people will develop an introverted personality. Not all victims become this way, but the introverts can be the most difficult to understand.

People with introverted personalities tend to keep to themselves. Over the years, they learn to withdraw into a shell of their own making. Only in this shell do they feel safe and protected. This does not mean that they can never form close personal relationships, but rather that it is often painful for them to do so.

They are not only cautious about expressing affection but are most comfortable when other people do not attempt to become emotionally involved with them. They not only are cautious about affection, they can be outright suspicious of it. This is the point when many will run away, as Judy did.

I know about this kind of suspicion. I was raised in an environment of "children are to be seen and not heard," and therefore I learned not to make waves or do things to call attention to myself. Normally my mother seemed to shut me out of involvement with her, but sometimes it appeared that she was inviting my participation in her life. Some question she asked, or a certain way she looked at me, caused me to make myself vulnerable by trusting her one more time. I would move close, open up, and confide to her some childish dream or desire. But she would turn that dream or that desire into something bad, and I would feel awful, wishing I had never mentioned it. Longing for intimacy with my mother, I followed this dangling carrot time after time, only to have it withdrawn—or, worse yet, slapped in my face—toward the end of the journey.

Looking back as an adult who has found healing, events like that can seem so insignificant. It is difficult in a way to realize how deep the hurts went and the painful repercussions they set off. I tried to ignore them back then, I tried to develop a tough skin, but the effects were still there.

To deal with such a person, we must have patience. We should do everything to show ourselves trustworthy, but we must choose our words and actions carefully. It is important to think about the effect our actions might have on this person.

Introverts can sit happily in a corner, content with observing their surroundings and not being an actual part of it. There are times, however, when loneliness almost overwhelms them and they long to be a part of others' lives. The loneliness inside their shell becomes more than they feel they can handle. But still, to come out of their shell is more painful than they can bear. They fear rejection. To be rejected is to be devastated. It hurts too much, so they dare not risk it. At this point they pull out their little bag of tricks and run away or slap others emotionally.

It is acutely painful and lonely to be on the outside looking in. Things always look sunny and perfect from the outside.

One winter evening, I was visiting with a friend who was a single mother. She was also a successful lawyer and owned a beautiful home in a nice section of town. As we sat down to dinner, all was not well. Such bickering took place among her and her teenage children. They showed little respect for each other. One son was developmentally disabled, which added to the confusion.

At one point I turned and looked out the large picture window to my left. Outside it was cold and the wind was blowing. I had an instant memory of walking down a sidewalk one dark winter night as a little girl. I looked at the warm houses as I passed by, seeing families gathered around the dining table, and my young lonely heart spun fantasies around these homes. Everyone looked so happy, content. So perfect! How I longed to be part of such a family!

I thought of that now, as I sat at this table with bitter arguing all around me. Things are not always as we suppose. People in pain do not understand this truth, however. The introvert, especially, can go into depression by comparing her circumstances to those of others.

But such a person can also experience the presence of the Holy Ghost a bit easier at times, since she tends to live a rather cloistered inner life. Shutting herself inside and shutting the rest of the world outside, she creates a quietness that can be conducive for communication with the Lord. But not always! Often, this person becomes so wrapped up in her own distorted thinking that the Lord cannot get through. He will stand at the door and knock, but negative, hurtful thoughts shut Him out. When we work with such a person—or if you are such a person—one of the first questions we should ask is, How is your relationship with Jesus?

Distorted Thinking
The introvert is especially susceptible to all types of

negative thoughts. These thoughts can cause the person to plummet into depression and despair. "I am hopeless." "Other people are better than I am." "I've tried so many times and failed, why bother?" "I'm afraid. . . ." Such people feel discouraged and inferior to everyone else, as though they can never measure up. No matter how accomplished they might be, there is always someone else who does more, and does it better, and therefore is better. When they compare themselves to an outgoing, extroverted person, they shrink up even more inside, feeling even more inferior. What may seem like snobbishness or lack of feeling is not really that at all. They often feel intimidated.

The extroverted personality, on the other hand, can wound the introvert without even realizing it. Extroverts typically do not want to hurt anyone, but their exuberant approach to life can be overwhelming at times. And to make matters worse, their enthusiasm at reaching out to include the introvert can cause the very hurt they want to avoid.

Extroverts have a way of overlooking the kinds of things that cause offense and hurt for introverts. For example, if they observe someone whispering, they do not stop to worry if they are being whispered about. Their optimistic nature tends to shrug it off with "So what?" Introverts, on the other hand, often take these kinds of things personally. If they overhear someone whispering, they may be absolutely certain they are being talked about! And this assumption can cause them to withdraw even more into their shell, hurt and bleeding from a wound that might not even exist.

If we can learn to let people be themselves, whatever that is, and just love them the way they are, then we can spare them—and ourselves—much disappointment. This is not to say that we want them to continue in behaviors that are potentially destructive. It is best if we can show them these things, but if for some reason we cannot, we can still go to God in prayer for them. We can talk to God about how we see these things. (After all, maybe we are not seeing them accurately.) And then, we must leave it to Him to do something about the situation. He can change people if they need changing and are willing to change.

It is not our job to change anybody. It is our job to love one another, accepting others where they are. After all, that is how God treats us. We come to Him in whatever state we are: "Just As I Am." We come to Him as sinners, and He loves and accepts us. Indeed, He loved us before we knew Him. He loves us too much to allow us to remain in our unhealthy condition, and therefore He seeks to change us from the inside.

Once we realize that it is not our responsibility to change others, we find a wonderful new freedom. We are free to accept people on their terms, love them, pray for them, and leave the rest to the Lord.

So, how can we help hurting people, and how can hurting people be healed? We must begin by exercising constant vigilance in our thinking patterns.

Extroverts must be careful with thought and word, always striving for "words fitly spoken." We should show kindness at all times to hurting people but should not push them. It may be that kindness will reach them at a period when they are longing to be included, and they will respond well.

If so, we can slowly include hurting people in activities and relationships. Again, we must not push them or rush them, but we must let them enter at their own pace. And should they withdraw after they have begun to enter, we must not get discouraged but just let them be. They need time and space to feel welcome. We should let them do the rejecting for a while. Patience is the key!

Introverts can try to develop the extrovert's "so what" attitude about many things. So what if someone might be talking about us? Our heavenly Father knows, and He can handle the problem. When something happens that seems devastating, we can ask ourselves this question: Will it matter in one hundred years? In fifty years? If not, we should let it go. Instead, we should focus our thoughts on Him!

If you are an introvert, keep your focus on Jesus. Try to draw a bit closer to the group each time you are part of an activity. Soon, you will find it easier to join the crowd. You will probably never do so with the ease of the extrovert. But it will become easier, and you will also find your new relationships to be a pleasant part of your life.

We just mentioned the necessity of changing our thought patterns. The way we think, to various degrees, emerges from our childhood. But we can learn to change the way we think, as we will discuss in a later chapter. For now, let us look at the interaction of cause and effect.

Chapter 4

Adultery

"And David's anger was greatly kindled against the man; and he said to Nathan, As the LORD liveth, the man that hath done this thing shall surely die . . . because he had no pity. . . . Now therefore the sword shall never depart from thine house; because thou hast despised me" (II Samuel 12:5, 10).

Uriah, the innocent party, paid with his life. David, the one who committed adultery, paid for the rest of his life. Adultery is a sin that has no winner. It is one of the most wretched sins, because it is committed against our own body. And God says, in the above verse, it is committed because "thou hast despised me."

Satan hates the church so much that he will do anything to destroy it. And what better way to wipe out families, cause ministers to fall, and break up entire congregations than by enticing people to commit adultery? Women as well as men have become vulnerable to this sin. One pastor's wife I know would have lost her soul because of this sin, except for praying friends who were able to touch God for her. God opened the eyes that the enemy had blinded. She humbled herself and repented, and has been restored.

Letitia has another victorious story. She dropped by one

morning just to say hello. We were enjoying the fellowship when, somehow, the conversation took a different turn. There she was, crying the way someone cries when she does not think she can ever stop. The floodgates had been opened. I sat quietly praying until the tears subsided.

I looked at this lovely young woman who was telling me about the time she lost her husband to another woman. Her face registered disbelief, even though the situation had exploded several years ago. Indeed, I remembered that when the same thing happened to me, it was months, years, before I could talk about it without crying. Thank God, this young lady had the Holy Ghost to help her through this! I did not know the Lord when it happened to me, but I realize now that the Lord knew *me*. He was there for me all the time, though I knew it not.

If your marriage is being threatened and you do not know the Lord, I hope you will take heart. Please know that He knows where you are. He knows your pain. He has a plan and a purpose for your life, and He will catch up with you and bring good to you!

Then Letitia turned her head and looked out across the field through my screen door. Her eyes looked as though they were registering the green grass, the tall and lovely trees, but I knew she was seeing and remembering the pain of long ago.

This was an ultimate kind of betrayal.

Rejection. Betrayal. Hurt. Infidelity.

"I called her up one day, Sister Allison, just to see how she was doing. This was before I knew about them. She'd been going through something, I didn't know what. So I called to check on her. I didn't know it at the time, but he was there—Kurt was there with her, even as we were talking! Listening to our conversation."

How humiliating! I felt the sting of betrayal afresh, for

this was an ultimate kind of betrayal. Rejection. Betrayal. Hurt. Infidelity. What is a man thinking about in a situation like this? What kind of feelings does he have toward his wife? Does he ever think of his wife as he woos the other woman? Does he ever feel a stab of regret, guilt, or sorrow?

People who have read some of my other books know my story and how this ultimate rejection ended with my swallowing over seven hundred pills. It was an attempt to end my life, because I could not face the pain, the emptiness of losing my husband. But pain is not meant to end in suicide. The purpose of pain is to draw us closer to the One who made us, the One who heals us and loves us, the One who has a beautiful plan and purpose for our lives. The purpose of pain is to be conformed to His image. (See Romans 8:17, 29.) We cannot be conformed to His image without enduring some suffering. In order for a lump of clay to become a beautiful finished pot, it must be battered and bruised and tossed around. When we have been tried, we shall come forth as gold.

Now Letitia looked at me with shock on her pretty face. "I trusted her, Sister Allison. I won her to the Lord! I trusted her!"

I felt like weeping, too. The friend she had won and trusted had shown her gratitude by turning around and stealing her husband. And now she sat with me, wondering how she could go on. My heart broke for the young friend in front of me.

I knew she would be all right. She had already survived the years of betrayal and the day he appeared on her doorstep wanting to be forgiven. She had taken him back, and although he still did not serve the Lord, she prayed faithfully, believing every day for his salvation. And I knew that God would honor the believing prayer of a holy lady.

A young man I will call Bob is a strong Christian whose goal in life is to be like Jesus Christ. He is a minister and one whose walk with God I admire very much.

Not long after coming into church, and before I met him, he won another young man to the Lord. Together they came to church, worshiped, and had fellowship together. Then one day, he learned that this friend was involved with his own wife.

The heartbreak that followed could have destroyed this young minister as he watched his wife leave both himself and his Lord. She took their child with her when she went, which made it even more devastating for my friend. But he had a God who never missed a thing. He had a God who felt the hurt, the injustice, and the irony right along with him. In the end, my friend was able to take this man to the altar and pray with him. From the depths of his being, Bob wanted his former friend to be saved. He lay upon the altar weeping with him, crying out to God to save and forgive them.

Is that what it means to weep with those who weep?

Is that what it means to forgive those who destroy and persecute us?

Is that what it means to love the way Christ loves?

Is that what it means to be a Christian?

Yes, a thousand times yes, to all these questions!

I learned a lot from Bob. He has taught me that maybe I did not really have it all together, after all. I know there is still so much of Jesus Christ to be developed in my own life. I get impatient; I want to be like Him *now!*

I have often wondered what Uriah must have thought when David brought him into town. There was no apparent reason for it. The Bible does not go into a lot of detail, so we can only surmise some things. But I wonder if Uriah suspected anything. As he lay at the king's door, did he wonder what he was doing there? And what David was doing at home? Did he spend a sleepless night? Did he wonder?

We can only speculate. This one thing I know: adultery hurts. It hurts everyone concerned. Most of all, it hurts our Lord Jesus. The passage of Scripture at the beginning of this chapter explains that we despise the Lord when we commit adultery.

Anyone who has been the betrayed, knows the agony of the sleepless nights. I remember lying in the darkness, one ear listening for the sound of the garage door opening and my husband's car driving in. I would doze and then jerk wide awake, looking at the clock. Early morning came and still no husband. This went on month after month.

I remember the imaginations in the dead of the night. While my children slept peacefully, often I would pace the floors for hours, drinking pots of coffee or bottles of booze. I wondered what I might have done wrong. How did I fail him? What did he need that I did not give? I thought of the hours of polishing floors and baking flaming cherry cakes . . . spit-shining shoes and starching collars . . . long walks in the park with the children explaining why Daddy could not be home. Was it enough? Where did I fail? Was I not the kind of lover he wanted? How could I have been better, more complete for him?

Slipping into the nursery, I would gaze upon my little son's sleeping face. "Where are we headed?" I would whisper to him by the soft nightlight. "Will I be left alone to raise you? What will you do without a daddy?" A little boy needs his daddy. Yet a part of me knew, even then, that the day would soon come when that little boy would be fatherless. Even right after his birth, as I lay in the hospital, his father was jetting down to Miami—to be with *her*. "I want the best for you, my little boy. But how much more can Mommy take?"

And I would visit my little girl, nestled in her room of lace and satin and western gear. She was Daddy's girl. Together they spent hours riding horses and raising show dogs. "What will happen to you, sweetheart?" Tears ran freely as I imagined her dreams of sugar plums but wondering if there were also dreams of fear and worry. Her little face was often wrinkled in worry and responsibility beyond her years. She knew about the other women. She had visited with them in their homes and at their jobs. She was being torn apart with wanting Mommy and wanting Daddy, too. Somewhere, deep within her ten-year-old soul, she must have sensed the evil of it all. And yet, she must have felt the need of denial, too, for how could a daddy she so adored do evil things?

Oh dear God, what we do to our children in the name of self!

The Mystery of Suicide

Through the years of a bittersweet marriage, I learned some things about suicide. Through the years, hopelessness led me to several suicide attempts. So I learned firsthand some of the things a suicidal person feels and thinks.

I discovered two main points about suicide: pain and punishment. Sometimes the pain became so bad, I could only escape it by a more immediate type of pain. A headache, for example, is forgotten when a paring knife cuts off a thumb.

One time the pain became too much and overwhelmed me. I had arrived home to discover him talking to *her*. I yanked the telephone out of the wall like a crazy woman and headed to the bathroom for a razor blade. Anything, I thought wildly, to shut out the pain! As the blade sliced into the tender skin, and the pain burned and stung, not only could I momentarily forget the pain of what my husband was doing, but I also had a sense of paying for whatever it was that I had done wrong. The blood was evidence that I was being punished—for whatever my failures were. Everything was being paid for by the carving of a razor blade.

Another time, when I was getting so-called rest in a

mental hospital, my husband phoned me. I stood at the pay phone in a room full of people as he began to explain to me that he would not be there if I came home this weekend. He was flying to Miami with *her*. My mind flashed to my babies! Where would my children be? My mind reeled between finding another razor blade and getting out of there, going home. I must have screamed.

No, he would not do this! Aware of eyes peering at me, I purposely and methodically placed the phone in its cradle and proceeded to the private office of my psychiatrist. I will get out of here! I told myself, He will not take my children into this! I rallied one more time and checked myself out of that mental institution that more resembled a resort hotel. Still, our days together were numbered. Only a few short months later, he made the final decision and was gone forever.

Now I can look back on those days and realize that all my sins were paid for—not by the blood that I myself shed in the wretchedness of a dark night—but by the precious blood shed by my Lord and Savior Jesus Christ!

Chapter 5

Alcohol and the Christian

"Every day in my line of work, faces go past my desk, faces filled with anguish and sorrow. I look deep into eyes that have long ago given up hope, and I yearn to reach out with the touch of my hand and make the pain go away. My heart yearns to roll up my sleeves and get in the gutter with these hurting, suffering people, and my deepest burden is for women whose lives have been destroyed because of alcohol."

I wrote those words at the height of my ministry to alcoholics in the early nineties. Although God has led me into broader areas of work since then, the words are still true.

Someone who is serving God and reading these words is toying with the idea of taking a drink. Perhaps to relieve the stress you are under, perhaps to try to dull your pain. Thank God, He sees you and has led you to pick up this book. I want to speak to you directly.

You tried to hide your tears from me, but I saw them anyway. Something in your spirit spoke to mine, and I recognized it right away. You are depressed, you are confused. Life has been hard on you lately, and you are feeling isolated and engulfed in your loneliness. I recognize the feeling; I have been there.

You call out to a God who seems silent. "Do you know my address, God?" you scream into the emptiness. And no answer comes.

Yet you know and I know that God is there. He has promised He will never leave or forsake us. But somehow—in some way—you need relief. Your faith in God is still there, in that you know He exists. But, somehow, in your despair, faith that He loves you—that He cares what happens to you—gets lost in a dark and heavy cloud.

I do not know how that first temptation will come to you. With Eve, her first mistake was to look at the piece of fruit, contemplate it. You might overhear someone extol the virtues of alcohol, how it can drown all your sorrows, help you to relax. If you ever hear such a statement, please do not listen! Recognize it as the voice of the serpent planting a thought in the garden of your mind. And then move on. Do not linger, do not even let yourself think about the possibilities. Because then the serpent will ask, "How can it hurt? One drink will only relax you. You deserve it." ("Ye shall not surely die.")

Somehow, I cannot escape the feeling that the serpent has already whispered to you. Somehow, in my mind's eye I see you poised there, delicately balanced between the Word of the Lord and the word of the serpent. Maybe your hand has already touched the fruit and you are pondering: "What would it hurt? I only need to cope, to forget the problems that are overwhelming me. Just for today!"

Snatch your hand away and fall at the feet of Jesus. Sometimes, when we do not hear from God in temptations like these, we erroneously assume it might be okay to go ahead and yield. But God did not make Eve stop, and He will not force you. He will let you make your own decision. Let that decision be to throw yourself at His mercy. That is where your help will come from.

I did not have anyone to talk to me like this, to warn me not to take my first drink. Oh, how I wish I had! But my first drink led to another. It always does, even when we *promise* ourselves it will not. Alcohol is one of Satan's greatest tools. It is sly and sneaky. I won't lie to you: it *does* feel good—at first. It *does* give everything a rosy glow—at first. It *does* make your problems seem to disappear—at first. That is Satan's way. It's called *deception*. We are *deceived* when we feel our problems no longer exist, because the next day—when the glow wears off—our problems are still there.

Indeed they are worse than before, because we have a hangover, or we threw away money that should have been spent on baby food, or we made an utter fool of ourselves, or we hurt a loved one who did not want us to take that drink, or we neglected some deadline.

My first drink led to others. Problems eventually came, and I was forced to choose between drinking and not drinking. By then I could rationalize everything away.

Beware! When you reach that stage, you are in serious trouble.

Please! Do not drink!

I see your shoulders sag. On your face is a look that is so familiar to me . . . helpless with a faint glow of hope. What else can you do? You have heard this before, but I will say it again: You have to give your broken life to the Lord. *But I have*, you protest. No, you have not. Because if you had, you would not be struggling with the bottle. Giving your broken life to the Lord means total surrender. It means doing His will. And what is that?

His will? Pray every day. Every day you must bring yourself to His feet anew to receive new strength. Prayer is the mightiest weapon on earth. Take your problem and your pain to Him. If there is anything you can do about a particular problem, do it. Otherwise, leave it in His hands—just until tomorrow! Let Him work on solving your problems today. Then tomorrow, when you come before Him again in prayer, pick up the problems again. But then leave them with Him again when you finish praying.

His will? Eat His Word every day. Saturate yourself

with Scripture. Sit down with your Bible. All the verses that touch your spirit, write them down on three-by-five-inch cards and post them all over your home and on the dashboard of the car. Have them everywhere so that when thoughts of gloom, despair, and doubt come, you have an immediate antidote.

His will? In everything give thanks. Let thanksgiving be continually on your lips. Count your blessings, truly. Look around you at all the good. The baby of a woman in my church was recently hit by a car. The baby recovered; it just had a small fracture. This sister had a choice: she could choose to dwell on the fracture, the hospital bill, the worries, or she could be filled with thanksgiving that the Lord spared her tot's life. She chose the latter.

His will? Control your thoughts. Think on true and honest things, as described in Philippians 4:8. Memorize this verse so that when the worries start coming you can immediately substitute good thoughts. For example, is it really true that your marriage is ending in divorce? You do not know that, not really. So do not dwell on it. Instead, think of the ways you can please your spouse. If there are things you can do—if there is definite action you can take—then do it. Do not imagine the worst. Instead, cast down imaginations (II Corinthians 10:5).

His will? Expand your world. Reach out to the needs of your family, to your brothers and sisters in church, to your classmates and neighbors, for they are hurting, too. Pray for them. Spend time thinking of kind and encouraging things you can say to others to help lift their load. "But," you may say, "their problems and pains aren't nearly as bad as mine." Really? Who is the judge of how deeply someone is grieving? If you are strong enough for God to allow the worst hurts and problems to come into your life, then you must be stronger than many others. You must be strong enough to reach out to those who are weaker and help to strengthen them.

As a final possibility, there can be a spirit of alcohol that roams around seeking whom he may devour. This spirit circulates among Christians in an attempt to lure them away from God. The Bible tells us to resist the devil and he will flee from us. We do not need to look for demons in every shadow, but we must be aware and alert. Often, too much attention and energy are given to evil spirits, but they are real. Spirits can attack individual and families, but we can stop this attack through the power of God.

Alcoholism ran in my family. But it does not have to pass down to my grandchildren. I have the blood of Jesus by which to break this cycle. I have power in the Holy Spirit to overcome this temptation so that my children are not immersed in this destructive lifestyle. I have power to bind the enemy in the name of Jesus so he will not harass my children in this matter.

Let us resist the devil and refuse to listen to him. Let us lift our heads as God's children, covered by His precious blood.

I remember when I used to drink. I would feel depressed, especially after a big disappointment in my life, and I thought I needed something to ease that awful feeling. So I would reach for a drink. Just one drink was all I needed; just to "take the edge off." Of course, that one drink led to another one, and so on, until I was drunk again.

But the times were few and far between when I could actually admit that I was drunk. Me drunk? Never! I had a few drinks, I thought—doesn't everybody? But drunk? No! I would get a chip on my shoulder, and all the anger I refused to deal with would cause me to drink again.

Our society has been deceived into believing that alcohol is harmless, when actually it is one of the most deadly, insidious drugs around. One of the reasons it is so dangerous is the very ignorance surrounding it. People consider it safe, so they drift into addiction with blinded eyes. "Everyone knows" heroin is a dead end, and we are starting to get smart about cocaine. But alcohol—most people think it is nothing serious.

They do not see the drunken woman in the dead of the night holding a gun to her infant's head. They do not know about the wife who just killed herself to escape the merry-go-round existence with an alcoholic husband. They shove aside the entire family that was killed on Christmas Day by a selfish drunken driver. They fail to make the connection between the beautiful lady in the hospital bed dying of liver malfunction and leaving behind a helpless brood of fatherless, motherless children. All because of alcohol. Not crack—alcohol.

Alcohol is socially acceptable. Alcohol is easily obtained. Alcohol is cheap compared to most other drugs. Alcohol is pleasant to take, easy to administer. It requires no needles, no special apparatus. But watch out. It will get you.

People say alcoholics can stop drinking anytime. I do not know what it is like to inject drugs into my veins, and I do not want to know. I do not understand that aspect of drug use. But I understand the internal condition. I know the hell that rages inside no matter how the drug got there.

I was a hopeless alcoholic for about twenty years. I crashed through the bottom before I started looking up, although that is certainly not a requirement. "Bottom" does not mean "skid row wino." Only three percent of all alcoholics fall into this category. They happen to be the most visible, so they are the ones people associate with alcoholism. But at only three percent, they certainly are not the typical alcoholic!

Women's Special Problems

There are a recognized five million women alcoholics in America today. That is admittedly a large number, so where are all these ladies? I used to be the group facilitator for the Drunk Drivers Program, but out of ninety group members, only five were women. So where are all the drunk ladies?

They are hiding. The stigma attached to women alcoholics is still very much in existence even today. And they not only are in hiding but are still being hidden by families and friends, people who feel they are doing the best thing for the alcoholic. (If you have alcoholic loved ones, the worst thing you can do is cover up for them! The sooner they face up to themselves, the sooner they can be delivered.)

I admire women like Betty Ford; the courage she displayed regarding her own alcoholism has done much good. Betty Ford, Joan Kennedy, Kitty Dukakis, and many other famous and well-bred women have stepped forth to acknowledge their problems with alcohol, shocking the world with the fact that alcoholism knows no sexual, social, or economic boundaries.

First, Admit There Is a Problem

It takes courage to stand up and be counted among the alcoholics. Alcoholics, already an insecure bunch, take enormous risks as they make this giant step forward. The battle for self-respect for a woman alcoholic has been an uphill, lifelong battle; it is ironic that one of the greatest strides forward in finally acquiring that long-coveted self-respect is found in the humbling act of simply stepping forward and removing the mask.

In my own case, I cannot begin to describe the *liberating* effect this disclosure had on me. I too wore a mask, even as a Christian. Not only had I been raised in an era when women had no right to drink, much less get drunk, but I was also raised in the Deep South. It is different there than, say, in California. To make matters even more complicated, I was raised by a blue-blooded mother who had been thoroughly schooled in ways to preserve the family name at all costs.

I am in a unique situation because I wear three hats. One, I was an alcoholic. Two, I was a professional in the field of alcoholism. And three, I am a child of God. When I tell the professionals that only God can deliver an alcoholic, they laugh. Most of them, myself included, were trained in humanistic schools, and so I am somewhat the maverick. When I am among Christians, my credibility is again at stake because a large bulk of the church simply does not understand alcoholism. There are so many preconceived notions, such as the skid-row thinking.

The typical Christian often ends up classifying all alcoholics as poor and uneducated, for example, when better than half are in managerial and professional occupations. In my own case, I was many things: an American student in Paris, a millionaire's wife, a magazine editor, a talk-show hostess, a chief executive officer, a graduate student, a psychotherapist, and so on—and all the while, a hopeless drunk!

Alcoholism Is Not a Disease

Alcoholism is not a disease, terminal or otherwise, that requires a lot of time and money to cure. Alcoholism is a *sin* that can be forgiven and wiped out in a mere instant by a loving God. And He puts joy and peace in its place.

I had a struggle with this concept at first. Having come from the professional ranks, I believed, like them, that alcoholism was a disease. But diseases do not keep us out of heaven, while drunkenness will (I Corinthians 6:10). Alcoholism can *cause* diseases, as other sins can do. But, thank God, it is no more a disease than gambling, cocaine addiction, or compulsive credit card spending.

Let us go a step further: alcoholism is not even the *problem*. Alcoholism is a *symptom* of a problem, a spiritual problem. That is why we must cooperate with spiritual laws if we are to get victory over it. God's laws are sound and solid laws that never vary.

I never cared much for beer, except as a teenager showing off how much I could put away in the beer garden at the military base. I loved manhattans and martinis. I put away fifth after fifth of Johnnie Walker straight and Hennessey's cognac. But beer is tricky. Wine is tricky. People can become alcoholics believing they are drinking something relatively safe.

Once a person is hooked on alcohol, ultimately only God can truly deliver him. An alcoholic's thinking becomes so distorted, so utterly sick, that before long and without any real awareness, he crosses a threshold and enters a realm beyond human aid. God can still help and will help, and He will use humans in the process. But the source of all ensuing help is the Almighty God. The sooner an alcoholic accepts this truth and begins to rely on God's power, the sooner he can start on the road to recovery.

The true alcoholic cannot quit drinking by mere willpower. Sometimes there would be no dinner on the table in my home because I was asleep—passed out. My children would be left in front of the TV without dinner. One night my six-year-old daughter decided to help out by popping some corn for her and her little brother's dinner. The place almost burned down that night.

The true alcoholic cannot quit drinking by mere willpower.

Was I sorry? Absolutely! I promised I would never do it again, and I really, truly meant it. I promised to quit once and for all, because, yes, I guess I did have a little problem in that area after all. Things went good after that—for almost a week. Then on came the pressure and out came the bottle. All I needed was one drink—I would just cut down, I did not have to quit, why be so radical! All I would have to do was cut back and not drink so much, and everything would be fine.

There is no way to describe all the horrors I went through. But the worst part is not what I went through, but what I put my family through. The ones I loved the most suffered so much, while I went my own selfish way, indulging and making excuses and lying and covering up.

It is a mistake to tell me, or any other true alcoholic, that willpower is all we need to quit drinking. First, we believe it, because we do not know any better. And that is the worst thing we could do, because when we try our best to quit and then fail, guilt and condemnation overtake us. We are sucked further in than ever before. Satan has his claws in even deeper. We cannot live with that kind of guilt and sense of failure. The hope of recovery slips through our fingers yet again, sometimes forever.

Another time, I thought I had licked my problem. I had gone months without drinking while pregnant with my son. After he was born, I continued not to drink and was convinced I was cured. My life was simply beautiful: a large suburban ranch, my dream house, country club membership, my personal Lincoln Continental, a private airplane of my own, live-in domestic help, my very own magazine and television show . . . but most of all, a husband I utterly adored and two precious children. I had it all, truly I did! If circumstances could cure alcoholism, then I would have been cured.

I was delirious with happiness. I let the housekeeper go because I was so jealous of my home I wanted to do it all myself. I was super mom and super wife. I spit-shined my husband's shoes, ironed all his shirts by hand, cleaned the floors with a toothbrush, and kept my children sparkling and bright. In addition to caring for my home, I wrote a book, directed a corporation, and carried an overload each quarter at the university. My husband said he was happy, and he *acted* happy. I was knocked off my feet when I made the fatal discovery that there was another woman.

I remember months of struggling, praying for miracles, going to Mass three and four times a day, hanging onto sanity only by splintering fingernails. Finally I went back on the bottle and took up where I left off. But alcoholism is progressive, which means a person does not quit and then start anew when he or she resumes drinking. My body and mind reacted as though I had never been dry, and I woke up in a hospital, bandaged all over. I had, for all practical purposes, quit living. And the tragedy was, the downward spiral was just beginning!

The doctors began treating me with all kinds of drugs. Soon I was so hooked on prescription drugs that I did not know if I was coming or going. I was taking about twenty-five pills a day of powerful, mind-altering drugs. I took a pill to wake up, a pill to go to sleep, a pill to pep up, a pill to calm down. But for the grace of God, I would have gotten so bound on street drugs that I never would have found my way back.

But God can speak to us in all situations. Sister Rosa, a lovely Christian in New Orleans, tells about her experience with drugs:

"I was addicted to drugs for twenty years until April 1990, when the Lord spoke to me in the back seat of a car while I was waiting for a drug transaction. I actually heard the voice of God say, 'No more, no more drugs!' I really didn't understand it, but I told my partners I wasn't buying and didn't want any more drugs, and I asked them to drop me off home.

"I knew of the things God could do, because I was actively involved in church work for seventeen years, yet still on drugs. I asked the Lord, 'What's going on?' For me to refuse getting high, I really thought I was tripping.

"Well, I went to church, had Bible studies, and

received the gift of the Holy Ghost in May 1990. The next month I was baptized in the name of Jesus.

"I told all my partners about my experience. I never had a high like I'm on now. I don't have to worry about hustling money to buy this high; I don't have to worry about the police or someone ripping me off while I am trying to get this high.

"What my testimony boils down to is that Satan tried to destroy me with drugs, but it did not work, steal my joy with depression but it did not work, and kill my body with sickness but it did not work. I am victorious in Jesus Christ, and if He can do all this for me, He can do all for you. He's not a respecter of persons!"

When we find ourselves in the realm beyond human help, we must look to God. Whether someone is on drugs or overwhelmed by the severity of life, the solution is to look to God. When we have to stretch up to reach bottom, we should look to God. When we truly reach the place where all resources are gone, He will step in and rescue us, if only we will look to Him.

I was yet to endure years of hellish nightmares before finally reaching that place. But finally came the day when I was all alone. It happens sooner or later, no matter who we are. I had blown another good job. I had abused my last friend. In my dark night of the soul, I cried out to God. I was desperate. There was nothing else to do. The Bible says to seek the Lord while He may be found. That was the turning point. God, in the form of the Holy Ghost, has transformed my life and the lives of my children. What I could not do, He did.

There is, I have learned, a big difference between merely "wanting to" and genuine, heartfelt desire. I wanted to quit for twenty years. But it took real *desire* to actually quit.

God gave me the desire to quit. I did not quit drinking by laying it on an altar somewhere. Some people have, but I could not. God did not deliver me at first. Even though I had always considered myself a Christian, I did not even have Him on my mind. But it was God nonetheless. He molded and remolded this pitiful vessel so many times! He chipped away . . . slowly, agonizingly . . . year after weary year. What an utterly useless hunk of clay I was to have required so much painstaking work on His part! After I no longer had alcohol, no longer had friends, no longer had pills, no longer had even the capacity to try suicide, no longer had any props or crutches, then and only then did God lead me to true repentance and into the dimension of His glorious and powerful Spirit. I am grateful beyond all words that He did not have to take away my children! They remained by their mother's side, faithful and loving to the bitter end, and for this I am ever in their debt.

Are you still toying with the idea of drinking? Have you begun that path and need to quit drinking? Are you doing drugs? Do you know someone who does? Pause right now, lay everything aside, and ask God to give you the desire to quit, to place it in your heart. Ask Him to lead you to someone who will help you quit. Believe that He has heard you. And then watch. He will act. Expect it! You can go through a dozen treatment programs, but unless you really desire to quit, you will not. Trust Him to give you the desire. Then follow where He leads.

God has led some to Alcoholics Anonymous or a sanitarium. I tried these and failed. He has led some to a medical model of recovery or a social model. I flunked these, too. But all of these methods have helped some people to quit. When I first quit, I was dry for about a year, but I was what the world calls a recovering alcoholic. I had to take one day at a time, fighting the urge to drink. I stayed dry; I did not give in and drink. But I was not happy and certainly did not have joy. I had quit the world's way. But there is more to life than that.

Perhaps God will lead you to Spirit of Freedom Ministries. The founder, Fred Hyde, has been where you are. He knows, and he understands. I was blessed to attend the same church with him for a while, and I learned that he can never give his testimony of what the Lord has done for him without tears. He knows firsthand about the supernatural, delivering power of the Holy Spirit.

The Spirit of God brings freedom—real, delivering freedom! God can remove all desire for alcohol forever. The world says, "Once an alcoholic always an alcoholic." That may be true in the world, but not in God's economy. I know what it is like to quit the world's way, and I know what it is like to be delivered. There is just no comparison! Once an alcoholic, always an alcoholic? No—not when we are delivered according to the laws of God!

What is deliverance? It is pure freedom. There is no longer a struggle with the old craving to drink, no living one day at a time. Deliverance means year after glorious year of not wanting to drink and not even thinking about it. And when you do, you are just so grateful that you are no longer bound that you simply want to give thanks to God, who has done this for you.

Demons can be involved with alcoholism. When I was gloriously baptized with the Holy Ghost in 1978, I was delivered from alcoholism. All desire to drink totally fled. But at that time, I did not even know what the baptism of the Holy Ghost was, much less what it could accomplish in my life. From time to time the old demons would come back to torment me with their lies that I was only a "recovering alcoholic," who must struggle the rest of my life, forever fighting that awful, dreaded "disease."

But it does not have to be that way. I do not stay sober by working through steps. I stay sober by the power of the Holy Ghost. Should He choose to remove His Spirit, I could once more become that old hopeless drunk, seven times worse than ever before. But His grace is truly sufficient!

I am not "unhappily sober," neither am I a "dry drunk." I know very well what these terms mean, because I have been there. I am simply a sinner woman on whom God took pity. I am simply dependent on Almighty God, and that fills my heart with unspeakable joy. I am most blessed of all people, and I am utterly thankful to my Savior for cutting the chains that held me bound. I am free!

I love you. But most important, Jesus Christ loves you. Even now He is reaching for you. Sometimes He stands back in the shadows to let us walk on our own. If He held us up all the time, we would never learn to walk. But even though we cannot feel Him or see Him, He is there. He cares. He is watching, and He is on your side. He hates alcohol and wants so much better for you. You can make it without alcohol. God will be on the scene! Wait and see!

Resources

- Spirit of Freedom Ministries. Its twenty-four-hour toll-free number is 1-800-535-6011.
- *Diary for an Alcoholic and Other Addict* by Lynda Allison. (Send $8.00, which includes postage, to Lynda Allison Doty, P.O. Box 1222, Bellevue, NE 68005-1222.)

Chapter 6

Depression and Suicide

Recently I read yet another article in our local newspaper that made me cry. It went like this:

". . . the death of a 17-year-old . . . from a self-inflicted gunshot wound. [A friend] said the teenager loved cheerleading, shopping and spending time with her friends. She was always there for her friends. She always had a smile on her face. . . . She was a good person, an all-American teenager. No one saw it coming. The young friend went on, however, to say that she realizes now there were signs that there was a problem. The teenager gave away her possessions, including a ring and several shirts."

Once I picked up the phone and heard: "I am afraid for his life, Sister Doty, I'm so afraid—"

It took me a moment to recognize her voice. She was not her usual happy self on the other end of the line that morning. Jan had been a friend for a long time.

"Who, Jan? What's the matter?"

"Brad. He's in such a deep state of depression, you just wouldn't believe! I feel like my heart is breaking. I don't know what to do."

As I listened to her talk, I realized I had heard a similar story already. Depression abounds! People are killing themselves, going into mental institutions, breaking up their homes. Sin abounds!

The following is taken from a letter written to me:

"I had been walking with the Lord for ten years. During this time, I was always able to overcome it [depression] through prayer and determination. But about six months ago, I could feel it again, trying to attack me. But this time it was different—I couldn't even pray! I couldn't even call on the name of Jesus. It was so hard for me to hold on! I took physically sick and was put in the hospital. In the past I had been in a mental institution and had tried suicide. I was so scared it was all coming back!"

Thankfully, this young woman was delivered in time. Many are not. I hear all too often about precious saints, ministers, and ministers' wives being taken to mental institutions and worse. Suicide is becoming a more frequent "way out." Suicide is a tremendously violent act. It is murder directed toward the self, like depression can be a form of anger directed toward the self. So many people who commit suicide do so out of extreme anger and rage that they have been unable to acknowledge and confess.

It is not unusual to be unable to separate depression and anger. For example, children may lose a parent or other object of love. Sometimes this occurs by death or separation but very often simply by the withdrawal of affection. Daddy is just not home. Mama is always busy. Learning to cope with grief is impossible because the children are unable to consciously acknowledge the loss. Instead, they interject the image of the lost person (incorporate it into the self) without assimilating it. The emotional energy associated with instinctual biological drives (libido) is withdrawn from the person and directed at the interjected image in the form of anger. Later in life, stress of loss can reactivate this anger and cause a kind of delayed grief. The accompanying self-criticism and guilt show that depression can be anger turned inward. In other words, the subconscious seems to be saying, "I cannot defile the name of my loved one by admitting my anger at him, so I turn it instead upon myself."

Because the grief has no conscious object, it is hard to dispel, and the symptoms of depression keep returning over and over again. A sister who battles with depression recently told me, "I have good days and bad days."

Cognitive therapists—of which I consider myself one, of sorts—believe that much depression originates in faulty thinking. Depressed people have become convinced, perhaps because of maltreatment by parents or later adversity, that they are unworthy, the world is hostile, and the future offers no hope. They give themselves no credit for success and blame themselves when things go wrong; they overrate the importance of every misfortune. They are vulnerable because they insist on interpreting everything negatively. This concept of depression is the basis for a popular form of psychotherapy.

Studies and research have shown that depression can be inherited. Is it caused by something within the genes, or is it something learned from others? It could be both, but also it could very well be a satanic attack. Spirits often attack families, leading one family member after another into sin. Suicide, incest, and alcoholism are common examples.

Behavior can be learned. For example, children learn to respond to a depressed parent by exhibiting the signs of depression. They instinctively learn to whisper, to frown, to let the young faces reflect the kind of sympathetic expressions that the depressed parent needs to see. These mirrored expressions of depression can become a way of life.

I know it was true in my own case. When I was growing up, my mother was often sick. The house had to be kept very quiet and still when she was bedfast. Depression seemed to lurk in every darkened corner. When she was sick, I was not usually allowed to see her. When she did permit me to come into her room for a few minutes after school, I soon learned that if I was happy she felt I was not concerned about her. In my efforts to please her, I became like her—depressed. I was not aware of the mechanics of what was happening, and they became "me." I learned to think of myself as depressed, worried, anxious.

My mother's sister, my beloved aunt, committed suicide. She had been one of those people who, like the seventeen-year-old in the news story, always had a smile on her face. We did not suspect anything until suddenly one day there came the phone call that she had shot herself.

People who have read my books are familiar with my attempt at suicide by taking seven hundred mind-altering pills. When I methodically swallowed those things, it was with the full intention of never waking up again. The Lord was gracious and faithful to this wayward child, however, and saw fit to spare my life. Although I did not appreciate it at the time, I have come to be thankful beyond anything words can describe. I know that, were it not for the mercy of God, I would be in hell this very minute instead of writing these words. That is such a humbling, awesome reality to ponder!

After the breakup of my marriage and the serious suicide attempt from which I was miraculously rescued, depression remained my companion. The years came and went, years dominated by an emptiness that I could not seem to fill. I was an achiever, a worker, a perpetual student. Still I found nothing to help me feel the completeness my soul longed for. Depression followed every accomplishment and every perceived failure. Depression dogged my every footstep, year after empty year.

What is depression, and how do we recognize it?

Symptoms of Depression

The person who is afflicted with depression gradually ceases to function. Symptoms include a change in appetite (either not eating or eating constantly) and a change in sleeping patterns (difficulty in sleeping or sleeping too much.) When I struggled with depression, my sleep patterns vacillated between the two. A typical sleep pattern is to fall asleep for an hour or so and then wake up, unable to sleep for the rest of the night. Another symptom is a change in crying patterns (crying all the time, feeling the need to cry but being unable to do so, or not crying at all when it would be normal to do so).

Numbness of affect (emotional feeling and expression) is common. A depressed person may sit staring blankly into space with a certain vacant look in the eyes. There is a shutdown of feelings and emotions. The person just does not care anymore.

A depressed person is unable to make simple decisions. In my own depression, washing the dishes would seem such an overwhelming chore that I kept putting it off until the sink was overflowing. I could not decide whether to load the dishwasher or do them by hand, so I ended up doing neither. Making the decision was just too tough.

A depressed person begins to lose interest in her surroundings. Things once important do not matter any more. Diane and Tim had been planning their vacation for eight months. Excitement mounted. But the week before time to leave, Diane found herself dreading her vacation. She had no interest in it, and packing and preparing became an overwhelming burden. She was a victim of depression.

When I suffered from depression, I went around feeling numb, robotic, going through the motions of living, not really caring about my surroundings. Attempted suicide was a crime back in the days I did it, so the authorities sent me to the mental hospital. There the staff filled me with all the pills I had so recently taken—their attempt to "cure" me. That was how I had obtained all the pills in the first place.

While in the mental hospital, I embarked upon what was called a "token economy." I was rewarded (given tokens) for all the "good things" I did, and I was punished (had tokens taken away) for the "bad things." I did not care for makeup, but in the hospital I would receive tokens every time I put on lipstick and other cosmetics. The staff interpreted the wearing of makeup as a sign that the person was getting interested in life again. I wore it heavily because I tried to get enough tokens to go home on a weekend pass. I did not care one bit about my surroundings or how I looked. It was all a pretense to earn tokens. To me the experience felt like a Girl Scout camp. I told them so. (And immediately forfeited tokens!)

Whether by behavior modification (of which the token system is a part) or psychoanalysis or other kinds of psychotherapy, the goal is to "reprogram" the patient.

Where Do We Go From Here?

My own background is one of abuse, including spiritual abuse by some teachers and preachers, but I did not need to be reprogrammed—I needed a deep healing by the Holy Ghost and people to love me back to health and trust. God provided all I needed without any outside "reprogramming." In the past, psychological methods had made me feel better—for a while. Then either the same old symptoms returned or new symptoms came, caused by the same deep hurt that had not been touched by the Holy Ghost. All I had was Band-Aids on broken bones.

From love flows all the other tools—prayer, compassion, reaching out to others, seeking them out, and leading them into the kingdom. And the pathway to love is through brokenness. We must be broken. Even as we lie before the Lord crumpled and broken, we must ask that He break us again.

Once when I went into therapy I was asked to work on my relationship with my mother. Throughout my life, our relationship had brought me much anger, guilt, and frustration, and I had never dealt with these emotions. Now I was to express them all, let out all the anger, and direct it toward my mother, who lived three thousand miles away. I was to shout and scream; I was to pound a pillow and beat things, all the while pretending it was my mother. Something inside of me warned against this kind of "therapy." I have since learned that our thoughts are very real things, and expressing raw anger in this way would not only have *not* helped me, it would have hurt my mother and me. Although I did not understand why at the time, somehow I sensed that this kind of thing was wrong. I certainly was not a Bible reader at the time and did not know that the Bible teaches the importance of pure thoughts and words. Our words are very powerful, and they are very real.

Thoughts—especially thoughts powered by strong emotions—are also real entities. Once set in motion, they continue to live. Speaking them is like adding fuel to the fire. What I needed to do was confess those things I was truly guilty of, and forgive my mother for all the rest. She was trying to cope with the problems of a sinful world and a fallen nature, just as I was. Understanding that principle is half the battle in cementing our relationships.

A minister and his wife came to me because the wife was so depressed she was having a nervous breakdown. As is my custom, at the end of a session I assigned them homework. It involved prayer and Bible study. The next time we met, they had not done their homework. They felt the assignment was too long. I probed a little bit to discover they were spending *no time* in prayer and Bible reading. How long can an automobile run without gassing up? And so the next week they had this daily assignment: fifteen minutes of prayer and reading one Bible chapter.

The next week their homework remained undone. This told me the problem went deeper than just having no time. Often, personal devotions and family life get pushed to the side in order to meet needs of the church. We all need to be careful in this area, because when we let our personal devotions slide, one day we will wake up to realize we are not spending any time in them. I cannot give spiritual counseling successfully if a person will not read and study the Word. Traditional psychotherapy is like giving an aspirin for cancer. The Word of God roots the cancer out. That is where help lies. Jesus told His disciples, "Ye are clean through the word" (John 15:3). We have to be willing to spend time with God's Word.

The more we get into His Word, the more we come out of ourselves. Jesus spoke about finding our lives as we lose them. In order to get victory over depression we must change our focus—off self and onto others.

I once had a pastor who struggled with depression. When I went to him for help, he gave me a prescription so simple I almost did not even try it. We were in revival at the time with an evangelist. My pastor's prescription for my depression was to bake a cake for the evangelist. I did not feel like going into the kitchen even for a cup of soup, much less to bake a cake. Depressed people do not have the energy to bake a cake! But I took the advice and baked the cake. It worked. It always works when we get outside of ourselves and focus on someone else. It is the devil's job to see that our spiritual eyes remain turned in to ourselves. That short-circuits God's work.

As you continue through this book with your Bible in hand, you will discover other wonderful insights for overcoming depression. Hang on, and let us continue our journey together.

Chapter 7

Wives Who Hurt

"Let not my lord, I pray thee, regard this man of Belial, even Nabal: for as his name is, so is he; Nabal is his name, and folly is with him" (I Samuel 25:25).

The headlines were startling, yet they are becoming more commonplace every day: "Man slays wife and two children, turns gun on self."

They say it does not happen in the church. This was in the church.

And then this, from *Omaha World-Herald*, September 22, 1997: "She kept believing her husband could change. On the morning of Jan. 8, 1988, her husband, Terry, opened a sweetheart card from her. 'Things are going to work,' it said. 'Let's just hang in there.'

"'It was so like her,' Terry said recently. 'She always had hope for me.'

"But there wasn't hope. The night before he found the card, he had shot Hazel to death and stuffed her body in a cardboard box in the basement of their home."

Here is another case, closer to home. We were sleeping peacefully about 2:00 AM, when there was a horrible pounding on the door. I was staying with a sister as an overnight guest, and we looked at each other, sharing a sense of danger. Leaving the lights off, we warily made our way toward the sound. As we cautiously peeked through the door we saw Sister Lorene, one of the sweetest ladies anyone could ever hope to meet. Quickly and furtively, she pushed through the door. "Please! Let me in! Billy's after me!"

I reached for the light and she stopped me. "Don't! He'll find us!"

We helped her over to the couch, where she sat down shakily. The streetlight on the corner shone brightly, and as my eyes became accustomed to the darkness, I could make out her face. She was covered with bruises and the smell of smoke. Across her face were tracks of ashes. Aghast, I asked, "What happened, Sister Lorene?"

Sister Lorene proceeded to tell us, through sobs and a fearful choking, how her husband, Billy, had started beating her again, this time with a fireplace poker. He was an abuser. This had been going on for years. He would get drunk and his wife would become a punching bag. He had never received the Holy Ghost, and he let everybody know he had no intentions of doing so. He made known his disdain for religion loud and clear. Sister Lorene had suffered in silence throughout the twelve years of their marriage. Now, the time had come for her brothers and sisters in Christ to become knowledgeable and, hopefully, to help.

Suddenly there was another terrible knocking. It was Billy! Sister Lorene froze. We all froze. "I know you're in there," his drunken voice hollered. "Open this door or I'll break it down."

The Extent of Domestic Violence

At some level most of us realize that domestic violence is a real problem among worldly people. It is one of those things that most of us prefer to turn away from. It is difficult to understand, and it is painful to contemplate. And there is an awful feeling of inadequacy. But more and more we have been forced to face the severe damage that this kind of abuse can cause—damage not only to the physical body but to the soul and the spirit of a person. What tremendous pain and scarring is done to a precious soul!

How many times this scene goes on in the church, we have no idea. We can look at the pretty lady at the end of our pew and bask in her smile, never realizing she carries bruises and cuts beneath her long, holy sleeves. Often, people like her just quietly slip away from us and disappear into the awful web. This is Janet's story. I know Janet, and I know her parents. What she relates here is true.

"A year after marriage, I just couldn't live for God anymore. Things went from bad to worse after that. I stayed with this marriage because of my child and my teachings from childhood. As my life went on, I learned to shut God out. My marriage during these years was rocky. My husband would go into a flashback from drugs and beat me till I couldn't walk. I have permanent damage because of him hitting me. He beat my head into a tile wall till he cracked my head open and knocked me out. He beat me till my eyes were swollen shut. My body took this abuse for several years. He abused me physically and mentally and would cut me with a knife at my throat."

Unfortunately, the sins of the world do affect the church. Not too long ago, a young mother told me how her husband started molesting their little baby girl. We need to keep our eyes and ears open and be alert!

Dr. Robert McAfee, a past president of the American Medical Association, has led a national initiative to improve the medical community's response to domestic violence. On October 15, 1997, in Omaha, Nebraska, Dr. McAfee assured health-care workers that they can make a difference in their battered patients' lives. A study several years ago found that more than eighty percent of abused women wanted to talk to their physicians about the violence they endured. The health-care workers were told that asking patients about violence should become as commonplace and natural as talking to them about a history of chicken pox.

Dr. McAfee went on to say that, in the past fifteen years, the number of women and children killed in their homes by someone who supposedly loved them equaled the number of American men killed in the Vietnam War. Imagine, he said, another wall like the Vietnam Veterans Memorial in Washington, D.C.—this one filled with names of those murdered by a partner, spouse, or parent!

If the medical community is trying to rise to the occasion, how much more the church of the living God! How much more should we be willing to listen and ask and talk. How much more should we be willing to help.

In Omaha recently, a funeral was conducted for a policeman who died after intervening in domestic violence. Omaha is making an all-out effort to combat this terrible sin, and I pray that more cities around the world will follow suit. But the efforts came too late for three Omaha-area women. Debbie of Papillion died in July of burns from a house fire her husband allegedly set. Annie of Omaha was found dead in April, strangled and beaten with a hammer. Her husband was charged with her murder. Frances was shot to death in April by her husband, who then killed himself. (See *Omaha World-Herald*, 21 September 1997.)

The same issue states: "Children witness an estimated 85 percent of domestic violence incidents, according to a study by the Women's Fund of Greater Omaha. A 5-year-old girl holds a Polaroid picture of her mother's bruised face, taken by a police officer called to their home."

Dr. McAfee talked about how doctors can create an

atmosphere in which battered patients feel comfortable talking about violence. He advised asking questions such as these: Do you ever feel afraid of or threatened by your partner? Has your partner ever destroyed anything you cared about? Has your partner ever prevented you from leaving the house, seeing friends, getting a job, or continuing your education?

The Husband Who Will Not Lead

But if any provide not for his own, and specially for those of his own house, he hath denied the faith, and is worse than an infidel (I Timothy 5:8).

Sharon stood in front of the bathroom mirror, watching her reflection. She was feeling that same old feeling again—she ached to walk out on her marriage. It would be so much easier, she felt, just to raise her children alone than to put up with Bob. He was a bigger baby than either Ashley or Ann. More than anything, Sharon wanted a godly home. She wanted a husband who would lead his little flock, provide for them, be the spiritual head. She had been bringing home the bacon the entire time they had been married—bringing it home, then cooking it in a pan. She was tired. Sharon was very tired.

As she brushed her lovely long hair, her mind went back to that morning. Their refrigerator had been on the blink for six months. Many pounds of meat had spoiled, and much food had to be thrown away, because the refrigerator was not dependable. She had sacrificed grocery money several times to have the repairman come out, and each time it had not really been fixed.

And now, God had been so good! A family in the church had decided to get a larger one, and they were giving their old one to Sharon. The only thing was, Sharon had to get it picked up and brought home. Bob had been promising for almost a month to get it. Each time he had failed, and then little Ashley had gotten sick because her milk was bad. Sharon could almost feel her blood boil.

Instead of working, he could be found at the church "praying" and "doing the Lord's work." He had lost all his jobs because of not showing up at work, or else he would quit. He just could not, or would not, hold a job. Sharon's blood boiled as she thought about it: in the eight years of marriage, he had never held a job longer than three months.

She opened her Bible to the chapter she had such trouble with—Ephesians 5. "Wives, submit yourselves unto your own husbands, as unto the Lord." Sharon closed her eyes. "But, Lord," she cried in a whisper, "what if the husband is always so wrong? Bob has made so many mistakes, and Ann and Ashley have been the ones to suffer for them." Sometimes the anger seemed to overwhelm Sharon. She almost hated him at times for what he did to her little girls. They were so small, two and four, and innocent. They did not deserve to suffer because of their daddy's foolishness.

"Husbands, love your wives, even as Christ also loved the church, and gave himself for it." Hah! She laughed bitterly. Bob would never give himself for anybody or anything. Self was his god. His god was his belly. "So ought men to love their wives as their own bodies." Sharon felt tears sting her eyes as she longed to have her husband love her! "For this cause shall man leave his father and mother, and shall be joined unto his wife." Sometimes the ache deep down inside her seemed unbearable. She was not unreasonable to desire this kind of husband. It was God's plan. "Oh, dear Jesus," her heart broke. "Give me strength to go on."

Sharon would just have to keep on keeping on and hang on some more. After all, Bob was changing. It was slow and painful, but she could see that God was answering prayers. God was so faithful. If only she could hang on long enough. Her nerves were frayed. Her body and mind were tired. "Help me, Lord," she cried into the still afternoon air, "help me to hang on."

A Grandmother's Pain

Mariette felt like throwing the phone across the room, her anger bordering on rage. Her daughter on the other end of the line had just let something slip that made her want to scream. She tried to pray, but all she could do was yell at God, "I hate him. God, kill him; get him out of their lives!" It broke her heart in two to see how her son-in-law was abusing her daughter and her grandchildren. Was there nothing God could do? Why, oh why, was He letting those innocent little babies suffer so?

Gary had never provided for his family. Rent, food, and utilities had always been paid by Carol's little home business. Mariette remembered many days watching Carol work at her typewriter while little fingers pulled at her skirt. Carol had five children, and the family was in church. Mariette thanked God for that! But what a hypocrite her son-in-law was, aspiring to be a preacher and tearing Carol down day after day.

Carol had been home-schooling the children for the past five years. And now he informed her that she was too stupid to home-school and he wanted them put into school. He had spit at her, "You never discipline the kids!" and "You're not teaching them right!"

His idea of discipline was beating them into submission. His idea of helping with homework was to beat the knowledge into them. And now the latest news was that he was leaving Carol. If that were not bad enough, he was filing for custody of the children. He had been building his case for a long time. The other woman was helping him. Mariette could not stand it. Only God knew how much Carol loved her babies, how much she had sacrificed for them. On those nights when he was out with *her*,

Carol was bathing fevered brows and calming childlike fears.

"O God," her broken grandmother's heart called out, "what can I do? I can't bear this!"

The Widow's Sacrifice

For all they did cast in of their abundance; but she of her want did cast in all that she had, even all her living (Mark 12:44).

She was one of those dear old saints of God, especially precious. Her time on earth was getting short, and she was ready and eager to go on to be with the Lord. But until that time, she kept busy and active. As a matter of fact, she was so spry and spunky I had a hard time keeping up with her.

One time when she was helping out in our first-grade Sunday school class, she learned that my story the following week was to be about the widow and the mites. Her old eyes lit up. "I've got an actual coin, would you like to show it to the kids?" Of course I would! So she spent that week digging out her genuine old mites, and when it was time to pass them around for the class to see, I watched her excitement. Memories danced in her eyes like a campfire, along with the satisfaction of knowing she was making a worthwhile contribution to these children's lives.

I knew something about her background. I had heard from her grown daughter how she had taken food from her children to give to a needy family. It was not so much food that it would be missed or cause her own children to starve, but taking a little bit from each child helped the hungry children next door. And it taught them how to give, by example.

Her life had been one of the most sacrificial I had ever

heard of. I knew about the abusive husband who forbade her to go to church. But, loving God as she did, she devised ways to get to church in spite of the obstacles. Stay home and miss church? Never!

There were times when she spent the afternoon preparing his dinner. She would set the table, get dressed, and put his dinner on the table. As he came in the front door, she would go out the back, down the street and to the revival service. She told me men would let some things slide if they had a full stomach.

I knew about the abusive husband who forbade her to go to church.

But there were times when the full stomach was empty before she came sneaking back in. He would be slumped over the kitchen table, bottle in hand, one ear out for the sound of the doorknob. And then a brutal beating would follow. "How dare you try to pull one over on me!" But no beating on earth could keep her from the house of God. No sacrifice was too great to be in the presence of the King.

I compare my life to hers and I wonder, Just how much am I willing to sacrifice? How much inconvenience am I willing to endure to help someone else? How willing would I have been to give up my children's food for the work of God? What do I really know about giving until it hurts? Jesus did. He gave His life. He continues to give and give to us, and He deserves our very best. Does He get my crumbs?

We should search our hearts and see what our relationship with the Lord really means. When we say, "Send me, Lord," are we willing to be sent next door in the middle of the night? I do not want to give my crumbs. My heart yearns to give of my substance, like the widow Jesus spoke of, who gave her very living.

Lord, I'm willing! You can take what is wrong and make it right.

The Hidden Victims

Tommy and Debra are little children who remind me of frightened birds—frail, nervous, insecure. Their dad is a heroin addict. Their large sad eyes reflect sorrow far beyond their years. They look like small old people! While Tommy's friends are getting a safe night's sleep, he cringes under the bed, trembling in terror. Tommy carries physical scars of terrible beatings from a drug-crazed father, beatings heaped onto an innocent, confused little boy for no reason other than that he is helpless and cannot fight back. Tommy is learning what real fear is, what it means to know despair. He is also learning the drug lifestyle. He is only seven years old.

Statistics tell us children like Tommy and Debra will grow up to become users and probably addicts. Is there not some way to break this dreadful cycle? Average Brother Christian sits helplessly on the pew. He does not feel that the issue affects him, so he is not motivated. Or maybe he is motivated but does not know what he could possibly do about it. After all, he is not a trained counselor. But the drug problem affects every Christian. It invades our lives, the lives of our children and our grandchildren. We cannot escape the problem of crime.

Over eighty-five percent of those in jail and prison are there at least in part because of alcohol and other drugs. Awful, ugly crimes are committed with that primary evil influence behind them! Drug use is undoubtedly one of Satan's chief tools of the hour. There is no way we can remain unaffected; drugs are invading our lives whether we are aware of it yet or not. And the field of substance abuse is a wide-open mission field!

People like Tommy's dad inspire contempt in most of us, and those feelings do not create motivation to help people like that. But God loves them. God is reaching for them. And if that is not enough motivation, we should think of the little victims, the women and children, who are being destroyed. Drug use is a complicated problem. When we deal with the alcoholic or other addict, we are not dealing with one individual but with a whole array of broken, suffering lives.

Satan hates the family. He works to exploit children, to cast them into a dark and ugly world of abuse. We know that there is an answer; His name is Jesus. He stands ready to help and to heal. He stands ready to show the way to a brand-new life. His love and His power can conquer the deadliest foe. The problem is, not all alcoholics and drug addicts are ready to meet the Savior. We can help them get ready, for II Timothy 2:25 tells us to instruct those who oppose themselves. Yet innocent people are suffering in the meantime. There needs to be a link somewhere, a step in between the addict who is on the street and the one who is at the altar.

That link is the church itself. We need a deeper commitment to the great commission and to prayer. Prayer changes things, it really does! Prayer brings addicts and abusers into the church, and prayer can keep them there.

Angela's Story

I have seen families delivered, time after time, through prayer. Here is a testimony from a woman who decided to stay and see it through. Angela tells us her story:

"After marrying without waiting on God, I began to reap what I sowed. I began to go through things in my marriage that I could not handle, but I still knew how to pray. Thank God for that. I began to learn and study about an unsaved husband and that he is sanctified through me. And God's Word says He'll save me and my household. I have had to stand on these promises when the trials began to come, when I saw my husband pulling one way and me another.

After two years of no communication, hardly ever seeing him, and his coming home drunk; hurt, anger, and bitterness began to build up, but I refused to give up and let the devil win the battle. I had God, and my mother and others were supporting and praying for me, assuring me that I could make it. God began to teach me to remove 'I' and self-pride, put flesh under subjection, fast and pray, hold my peace and let Him fight my battles. Soon I began to see results.

"My husband is not yet in the church, but I know God is dealing with him. We have decided to pray together. God is teaching me to be a loving and submissive wife and to let my husband be the man and take responsibility of his household. God is teaching me to stand still and wait on Him. He is not a respecter of persons, and He can do anything but fail."

I have seen God bring victory time after time. So many women have come to me on the verge of leaving home. Emotionally, they felt they could no longer handle the lack of leadership, the verbal abuse. I have seen them sit down with the Word of God and study what He had to say. I have seen them decide to stay home a little while longer and try to apply the Scriptures. And I have seen marriages saved because of this decision.

I see men preaching the gospel today because their wives chose to trust God in the past. Men are ushering, leading cell groups, serving God, and managing their homes . . . because of a wife who trusted God. Yes, God can do anything but fail!

Chapter 8

The Prodigal Child

I will never forget that day as long as I live. It was the day after Thanksgiving. I knew something was wrong with my son; I had sensed it for some time. But he no longer lived at home, and we did not attend the same church. He had indeed made himself scarce, and now I was hearing the dreadful reason why.

I looked him in the eye and, as much as I dreaded the answer, asked, "Have you quit church, Joseph?" My mind was reflecting on the powerful way he had served God—as department head, district paper designer, gifted musician, you name it—so talented, with such a big heart for God. Now I waited for his answer.

He hemmed and hawed a few minutes, then confessed. Only if you have learned this truth about your own child can you understand the shock, the sorrow, and the terror I felt.

I squeezed back the tears. They would only make the matter worse, some part of me realized. And so, numb all over, emotions frozen, I made my way out of his presence and to my own home. It was only then that I allowed myself to vent my pain.

It hurts to know your children might be lost. It does not matter if they are five or fifty, you love them. You care! It breaks your heart to see how they are living. You look at the pew where they used to sit when they came to church, and your heart aches. It is so heavy. The emptiness you feel borders on despair!

You have said it all. They know the truth. There is nothing left to say, nothing left to do, except to pray. And trust God. He is all powerful. He knows how to reach them . . . in His time . . . not by our time clock. He sees inside the heart; He knows exactly what it will take to bring that wayward child home. We must trust Him and feed, every day, on His Word.

As I believe God for my Joseph, I believe Him for *your* child. Together, we can make a difference. Together, we can unite against the enemy and reclaim our precious children. Let us pray one for another and for each other's children.

We have no way of knowing when our lost one will come back. But we must believe. For a long time, I found it very difficult to believe. The circumstances I would see my son involved in belied the possibility of his returning to the Lord. I just could not see it, much less believe it!

And sometimes, just when it seemed that maybe my faith was starting to build up—maybe after he asked a certain question or behaved a certain way—then he would do or say something that sent my faith crashing. This was utterly frustrating. How, if my faith was involved, would my poor child ever be saved? I would cry out to God, "Lord, I believe, help Thou mine unbelief!" While that seems like such a hopeless prayer, it is a prayer that will build faith because it directs us to the only one who is Savior—the only one who can do anything about the situation.

The Lord began to work on my faith. "Faith cometh by hearing, and hearing by the word of God" (Romans 10:17). If nothing else good has come from this wilderness experience, it has given me a new devotion to the Word of God.

During my hours of prayer and study of the Word, I

compiled the following passages of Scripture, prayers, and encouraging thoughts.

- "A certain man had two sons. And the younger of them said to his father, Father, give me the portion of goods that falleth to me. And he divided unto them his living. And not many days after the younger son gathered all together, and took his journey into a far country, and there wasted his substance with riotous living. . . . And when he came to himself, he said . . . I will arise and go to my father. . . . And he arose, and came to his father. But when he was yet a great way off, his father saw him, and had compassion, and ran, and fell on his neck, and kissed him. . . . For this my son was dead, and is alive again; he was lost, and is found. And they began to be merry" (Luke 15:11-24). Reading this passage in its entirety helps us take heart. I pray, "Lord, help my child to come to himself."

- "Then Jesus answered and said unto her, O woman, great is thy faith: be it unto thee even as thou wilt. And her daughter was made whole from that very hour" (Matthew 15:28). The key is faith. We must keep our eyes on Jesus and off the circumstances. Peter walked on the water until he started looking at the circumstances all around him. Then he sank.

- "Therefore behold, I will hedge up thy way with thorns, and make a wall, that she shall not find her paths" (Hosea 2:6). I pray, "Yes, Lord, confound his worldly pursuits. Do not let his worldly ambitions be realized, Lord; confound them. Let them come to nothing."

- "Behold, I am the LORD, the God of all flesh: is there anything too hard for me?" (Jeremiah 32:27). Indeed! There is nothing too hard for our God!

- "God is in the midst of her, she shall not be moved: God shall help her, and that right early" (Psalm 46:5).

- "For the children . . . have only done evil before me from their youth, for the children of Israel have only provoked me to anger with the work of their hands, saith the

LORD . . . and they have turned unto me the back, and not the face: though I taught them, rising up early and teaching them, yet they have not hearkened to receive instruction. . . . I will not turn away from them, to do them good; but I will put my fear in their hearts, that they shall not depart from me. Yea, I will rejoice over them to do them good, and I will plant them in this land assuredly with my whole heart and with my whole soul" (Jeremiah 32:30-41). What love! What mercy! If ever there were a passage of Scripture to increase our faith, this is it! What a good God we have! We have all mistreated Him, yet still He has mercy and love. Oh, what a God into whose hands we can place our wayward children!

• "Fear not: believe only, and she shall be made whole" (Luke 8:50). Let us simply believe. Instead of trying to figure out everything, let us believe only!

• "Weep not. She is not dead, but sleepeth" (Luke 8:52). We know nothing is too hard for the Lord, but in our limited human thinking it seems easier to wake a sleeping person than a dead person.

• "This is the confidence that we have in him, that, if we ask anything according to his will, he heareth us: and if we know that he hear us, whatsoever we ask, we know that we have the petitions that we desired of him" (I John 5:14-15). If we ask according to His will, we have it. We know it is His will for our children to be saved, so we know that in response to our prayers He will move on their hearts.

• "I also withheld thee from sinning against me" (Genesis 20:6). There have been times when I could have sinned—probably would have sinned—but for a wrong number or a strange knock on the door. I pray, "Do that for Joseph, Lord. Please hold back my child from sinning. You knocked Saul off his horse. Knock Joseph off!

• "But the Lord is faithful, who shall stablish you, and keep you from evil" (II Thessalonians 3:3).

- "Now unto Him that is able to keep you from falling, and to present you faultless before the presence of his glory with exceeding joy" (Jude 24). He is faithful! He will establish!
- "The Lord will not cast off forever: but though he cause grief, yet will he have compassion" (Lamentations 3:31-32).
- "Fear thou not . . . saith the LORD; for I am with thee . . . I will not make a full end of thee, but correct thee in measure" (Jeremiah 46:28). I pray, "Correct him, Lord."
- "God hath chosen the weak things of the world to confound the things which are mighty" (I Corinthians 1:27). They may think they know it all, but God knows just how to reach them.
- "Not by might, nor by power, but by my Spirit, saith the LORD of hosts" (Zechariah 4:6).
- "My brethren, be strong in the Lord, and in the power of his might" (Ephesians 6:10). I pray, "Lord, help me to be strong."
- "According to his mercy he saved us" (Titus 3:5-6). I pray, "Jesus, he doesn't deserve it, but have mercy!"
- "I know whom I have believed, and am persuaded that he is able to keep that which I have committed unto him against that day" (II Timothy 1:12). I have committed my children to Him; I must trust that He will keep them.
- "We know that all things work together for good to them that love God, to them who are the called according to his purpose" (Romans 8:28). I pray, "Lord, help me to remember this principle. It's true! Remind me again!"
- "By grace are ye saved through faith; and that not of yourselves; it is the gift of God; not of works, lest any man should boast" (Ephesians 2:8-9). There is nothing I can do to save my son. So I will simply believe.
- "I will allure her, and bring her into the wilderness, and speak comfortably unto her" (Hosea 2:14). I pray, "Yes, Lord, speak with Joseph today."

- "He shall redeem their soul from deceit and violence" (Psalm 72:14). Joseph has been deceived by the enemy, but my God shall redeem him!

- "He shall not be afraid of evil tidings: his heart is fixed, trusting in the LORD. His heart is established" (Psalm 112:7-8). Even though the circumstances may look hopeless, I will not fear so-called bad news! No matter what, I am determined to keep loving God.

- "Ye that fear the LORD, trust in the LORD: he is their help and their shield" (Psalm 115:11).

- "Save now, I beseech thee, O LORD: O LORD, I beseech thee, send now prosperity" (Psalm 118:25).

- "Before I was afflicted I went astray: but now have I kept thy word" (Psalm 119:67).

- "Except the LORD build the house, they labour in vain that build it" (Psalm 127:1). We must allow the Lord to handle this problem, for we have a way of making things worse.

- "That our sons may be as plants grown up in their youth: that our daughters may be as corner stones, polished after the similitude of a palace" (Psalm 144:12).

- "Put not your trust in princes, nor in the son of man, in whom there is no help" (Psalm 146:3). We must trust in God.

- "The LORD openeth the eyes of the blind" (Psalm 146:8). I pray, "Help him see, Lord!"

- "He healeth the broken in heart, and bindeth up their wounds" (Psalm 147:3). I pray, "Heal my broken heart, Jesus, and heal the wounds of my dear children. Joseph was hurt very badly before he quit church. But you can help him to forgive, and you can bring healing to him."

- "Deliver my soul from the sword: my darling from the power of the dog" (Psalm 22:20).

- "And none can keep alive his own soul" (Psalm 22:29). None of us will ever get to heaven if we have to depend on ourselves. We must trust Him.

• "For thy name's sake, O LORD, pardon mine iniqui-ty" (Psalm 25:11). I pray, "For Thy name's sake, forgive my child, Lord."

• "Wait on the LORD: be of good courage, and he shall strengthen thine heart: wait, I say, on the LORD" (Psalm 27:14). We need to be still; He knows what He is doing.

• "None of them can by any means redeem his broth-er, nor give to God a ransom for him" (Psalm 49:7). We are not our children's savior—He is!

• "O turn unto me, and have mercy upon me; give thy strength unto thy servant, and save the son of thine hand-maid" (Psalm 86:16).

• "He shall save the children of the needy" (Psalm 72:4). I pray, "I have a need, Lord!"

• "The prayer of the upright is his delight" (Proverbs 15:8). We must keep praying, for He never gets tired of hearing us. In fact, He delights in hearing from us. I pray, "Help me to stay clean and pure, Lord, in all my ways."

• "I have seen the travail which God hath given to the sons of men to be exercised in it. He hath made every thing beautiful in his time" (Ecclesiastes 3:10-11). The work takes place in His time, not ours. We have to learn to wait on God. Waiting is the hardest work there is, at least for me. I would rather do anything than wait. But I do not want Joseph to pretend feelings he does not have. When he prays through to a renewal, I want it to be for good! I want him to be stronger than ever! And so I have to wait, so that it is all in God's perfect timing.

• "He shall feed his flock like a shepherd: he shall gather the lambs with his arm, and carry them in his bosom, and shall gently lead those that are with young" (Isaiah 40:11). I pray, "Feed my child; carry him, Lord!"

• "He giveth power to the faint; and to them that have no might he increaseth strength" (Isaiah 40:31).

• "For I the LORD thy God will hold thy right hand,

saying unto thee, Fear not; I will help thee" (Isaiah 41:13).

• "I will pour my spirit upon thy seed, and my blessing upon thine offspring" (Isaiah 44:3).

• "Behold, I have graven thee upon the palms of my hands" (Isaiah 49:16). He has also engraved my children on the palms of His hands! He will not forget them!

• "Who are kept by the power of God through faith unto salvation" (I Peter 1:5). Faith: there it is again.

• "I will contend with him that contendeth with thee, and I will save thy children" (Isaiah 49:25). God said that, not us! Demons who fight for our children are contending with us—and therefore with God Himself!

• "And all thy children shall be taught of the LORD, and great shall be the peace of thy children" (Isaiah 54:13). Sometimes the lessons of the Lord are hard lessons, but He is their teacher!

• "Let us therefore come boldly unto the throne of grace, that we may obtain mercy, and find grace to help in time of need" (Hebrews 4:16).

• "Now faith is the substance of things hoped for, the evidence of things not seen" (Hebrews 11:1). Though we may not see any evidence that He is working, and though it may look as if things are getting worse, we know He is at work. That is what faith is all about.

• "I and the children whom the LORD hath given me are for signs and for wonders" (Isaiah 8:18). God is the one who will get the glory out of the conversion of our children. The worse things become, the greater the victory will be!

• "For perhaps he therefore departed for a season, that thou shouldest receive him forever" (Philemon 15). Perhaps the things our wayward children experience in the world will bring them to God forever, and that is what we really want—their eternal salvation. For some people, their flesh has to be delivered to Satan so their soul might be saved. (See I Corinthians 5:5.)

• "In meekness instructing those that oppose themselves; if God peradventure will give them repentance to
the acknowledging of the truth; and that they may recover themselves out of the snare of the devil, who are taken
captive by him at his will" (II Timothy 2:25-26). I pray,
"Lord, help our children to recover themselves out of the
snare of the devil."

• "Giving thanks always for all things unto God and
the Father in the name of our Lord Jesus Christ"
(Ephesians 5:20). We are to give thanks for all things, not
merely in all things.

• "For we are saved by hope: but hope that is seen is
not hope: for what a man seeth, why doth he yet hope for?
But if we hope for that we see not, then do we with
patience wait for it" (Romans 8:24-25). I certainly am
hoping. I will patiently wait for the answer to come.

• "And they that heard it said, Who then can be
saved? And He said, The things which are impossible with
men are possible with God" (Luke 18:26-27). As I look on
things, I do not see how Joseph could possibly be saved—
things are just too bleak. But it is possible with God.

• "And behold, a woman of Canaan came out . . . and
cried unto him, saying, Have mercy on me, O Lord, thou
son of David; my daughter is grievously vexed with a
devil" (Matthew 15:22). This woman's daughter had a
demon, yet the woman was asking for mercy for herself.
That is how it is with backslidden children; parents need
mercy, too!

• "He is able even to subdue all things unto himself"
(Philippians 3:21). Even our children . . . in His time.

• "Then came she and worshipped him, saying, Lord,
help me" (Matthew 15:25). That is where we get our
answers—in worship. That is what Job did; he fell down
and worshiped.

• "And she said, Truth, Lord; yet the dogs eat of the

crumbs which fall from their masters' tables" (Matthew 15:27). I pray, "Lord, I know Joseph is sinful and does not deserve anything from You. But I ask You for Your crumbs, Lord—they will get the job done."

• "Let tears run down like a river day and night: give thyself no rest; let not the apple of thine eye cease. Arise, cry out in the night: in the beginning of the watches pour out thine heart like water before the face of the Lord: lift up thy hands toward him for the life of thy young children" (Lamentations 2:18-19). My child is the apple of my eye! The Lord tells me to intercede for his very life.

• "A voice was heard in Ramah, lamentation, and bitter weeping; Rahel weeping for her children refused to be comforted for her children, because they were not" (Jeremiah 31:15). We cannot be comforted until our children are returned to the fold. We must weep until then.

• "Thus saith the LORD, Refrain thy voice from weeping, and thine eyes from tears: for thy work shall be rewarded, saith the LORD, and they shall come again from the land of the enemy. And there is hope in thine end, saith the LORD, that thy children shall come again to their own border" (Jeremiah 31:16-17). My work is intercession for my children. God says that it will be rewarded. They shall come again from the power of the devil. They will come again into the church of the living God.

Chapter 9

∼

When "Gay" Hurts

At a conference recently, I was having dinner with a pastor from the South. Toward the end of the meal, she laid down her fork and asked: "Do you mind if we talk some business?" The pain was obvious on this dear pastor's face.

As she began to tell me about two women in her church, I could hear the grief in her voice. They had left their homes, families, and everything they once held dear and had run off together. A few days later they returned, repentant. They apologized publicly to the church and asked to be taken back into the fold. The request was granted and counseling was started.

Things appeared to be going along pretty well until, a few weeks into the counseling, the pastor discovered the women were drifting back into the behavior. She had tried everything and was at her wit's end. What could be done?

Some say things like this do not happen in the church. They say that as long as we are living for God, ugly things like homosexuality cannot touch us. They say that Christians are exempt from such things. Unfortunately, the sins of the world do affect the church. This chapter is written in response to the cries of many people who have discovered they must bear this kind of pain—usually alone—and they need to know how to cope. It is also designed to help those who might be called upon to minister to people caught in the throes of this awful heartache, either the homosexual himself or his loved ones.

We are living in the end time, and as in the day of Sodom, so shall it be at the coming of the Son of Man. (See Luke 17:28-30.) The spirit of homosexuality has been unleashed on the earth as never before. It is a powerful spirit. It is a very real spirit. We will be seeing it more and more in our churches. Hiding our heads in the sand will not make the problem go away. In my work as counselor, I am continually confronted with the knowledge that yet another brother, sometimes a sister, has become involved in homosexuality. Althea is an example.

Althea's day began just like any other day. She got up at six, made breakfast for Bill and the kids, got them off to school and work, and sank into the easy chair by the window for her daily devotions. Her heart was light this morning. It was storming and cold outside, but inside, by the light of the soft lamp, Althea felt snug and warm. She was content with her life, happy with the Lord and with her family. She was not prepared that morning for the beginning of the end of her beautiful world.

As she completed her devotions and placed her Bible on the end table, she saw it: a piece of paper or something behind Bill's recliner, across from hers. With a smile at her husband's carelessness, she reached behind his chair to retrieve a photograph. Althea gasped. A young man clad in a bikini was smiling into the camera. He was tanned, had white teeth, and was muscular. She frowned. Who was this? What was Bill doing with this picture?

Before dinner that night, Althea knew. As she held the picture out to him, Bill confessed to her. He was homosexual. He had struggled for years, he said, and for the past six months had at last become a practicing homosexual. He felt it would be best if they divorced. Althea felt heat, cold, and dizziness all at the same time. *Where had she gone wrong?*

Marvin's wife Marianne left him for another companion, a female she met on the Internet. Marvin, a minister of the gospel, was haunted by the question: W*here had he gone wrong?*

Suzanne's handsome young son announced to her one afternoon, "Mom, I guess you'd better hear it from me rather than someone else. I'm gay." Suzanne was devastated. Her child? Her own flesh and blood? She cried out to God in the darkness of the night, "My son, my only son! *Where did I go wrong?*"

> "Mom, I guess you'd better hear it from me rather than someone else. I'm gay."

All of these people were tormented by fears and imaginations and worried about what *they* had done to contribute to this. Each of them asked the same question: *"Where did I go wrong?"* What could *they* have done differently?

First, we need to understand that people in this situation have not done wrong. It is a pattern of response that when things do not go the way we think they should, we blame ourselves. One mother cried in my arms. "Was I too domineering?" she sobbed. "I've heard that domineering mothers make homosexual boys."

Most of the men I have dealt with, either directly or through their mothers, were boys who had been raised with father problems, not mother problems. Either the father was absent physically, or he was absent emotionally. When a boy's father is there for him, he usually does not have this kind of identity problem. He has the security of a father who cares, who models, and who gives him a sense of belonging.

A father who does not provide for those of his own household is worse than an infidel. Provision means a whole lot more than just paying for the groceries. The

101

Bible tells us that fathers must provide emotionally, spiritually, and mentally for their children. When a father fails to do so, he transgresses the law of God. This sets the children up for the enemy's camp. If Dad will not give what the child needs, Satan will be more than happy to provide a counterfeit somewhere along the line!

Boys with absent fathers desperately search for a father's love. They search for an identity. They often grow up surrounded by females and therefore become more familiar with the female than the male. In the normal pattern of maturing, girls gravitate to girls for intimate friendship, and the same for boys. Girls are familiar with girls, and boys are familiar with boys. Girls play dolls together; boys play army. Girls imitate Mama, and boys follow after Dad. This is the way things are meant to be. God created the two-parent family—not out of whim, but because it is what makes things work right.

When the boy and girl grow up and it becomes time to date, they are attracted to what is different, what is not so familiar. The girl seeks the boy, the boy seeks the girl.

But when there is no father for the boy to love and be close to, he seeks love from Mama and sisters and maybe sister's girlfriends. Girls become familiar. He becomes much more comfortable with girls as friends than boys. When it comes time for him to begin to seek out a mate, he may be drawn to the unfamiliar, in this case the male. Not everyone in this situation is drawn to homosexual behavior, and there are other interacting factors that help lead to this type of behavior, but often the situation we have just described is a key to understanding what has happened.

Satan's Public Relations Department

Satan is out to destroy marriage and the family and to discredit God in any way He can. He wants to destroy people, because God loves us so much. He wants to cause all kinds of confusion and sorrow. Then more people will point their finger at God and say, "What kind of God would let this happen?" They fail to realize that Satan is the one behind all the dysfunction in the first place. Satan is so jealous of God. He wants to destroy our love and trust and respect for a holy and loving God. One effective way is to instigate same-sex relationships.

Satan is sly. He has gradually extended his influence in this matter over the mainstream of America—including education, television, radio, newspapers, book publishers, and more recently, family-revered Disney.

It is surprising how much literature on the market promotes homosexuality. Much is written by so-called Bible scholars who twist every verse in the Bible on the subject to say what Satan wants it to say. For example, one book states, "Top scholars—such as Yale history professor . . . and New Testament professors . . . of Berkeley and . . . of Union Theological Seminary—show that those who perceive Bible passages as condemning homosexuality are being *misled by faulty translation and poor interpretation*" (Helminiak, 1994, emphasis added).

The foreword of this book says, "There is no book I love more . . . than the Bible. Yet, had I not escaped the literalism of my Christian upbringing, I could not make that statement, for long before now I would have either dismissed the Bible as a *hopelessly ignorant and prejudiced* ancient religious document or I would have *denied reality and become myself a small-minded religious bigot*, using literal scriptures to justify my prejudices. A literal Bible, in my opinion, admits no other options. . . .

"This author *goes beyond the literal words . . .* to enter into the spirit of the bible. . . . [He] dares to *set aside the culturally conditioned biblical words* for the power of his Lord . . . who embraced the outcasts of his society." There is no mention of the many warnings not to add or take away *anything* from the Bible!

The author explains, "As a Roman Catholic—and

more importantly, a *thinking person*—I do not *presume
the Bible provides the last word on sexual ethics. In
my mind, the matter is more complicated than that"*
(Helminiak, 1994).

One wife told me she desperately sought information
to help her cope with her husband's confession. She went
to the Bible bookstores, but not finding much material on
the subject, she sought out other bookstores. She found a
good-sized store that carried gay and lesbian materials
exclusively. She thought she would find what she needed,
because much of the material included "Bible" in the title.

She purchased a few books and hurried home to
begin her education about what went wrong with her and
her husband. But as she read, her heart broke. The books
spoke against her Bible and her God, undermined her
Christian faith, and attempted to destroy all that she held
dear. It called her names like "small-minded religious
bigot."

Walt Disney—what would he say and do, if he could
see what has become of his cherished family-friendly
company? Disney has gone so far off the deep end that
several large family organizations and church denomina-
tions have felt the need to boycott it. This information
comes from one of the family organizations:

"Disney is using its enormous influence to change
attitudes about homosexuality, destroy Christian beliefs,
and ultimately undermine the morals of American's children. Its sheer size and command of the media enable it
to convey their pro-homosexual, anti-God values to tens
of millions of Americans, and especially to children. For
generations, parents trusted Disney. It's hard to let it go.

"Disney boasts that it has more homosexual employ-
ees than any other entertainment company. They are
catered to with health and other benefits far beyond the
ordinary. Disney World annually hosts 'Gay and Lesbian
Pride Day.'"

Disney is also trying to "create" a "third sex," which they say should be acknowledged and treated the same as heterosexual males and females. But only God can create! And His day of creation ceased after making male and female. Even the animals were created by a wise and loving God in pairs of male and female.

Born That Way?

One of the most dangerous lies we have to deal with is the notion that a homosexual is "born that way; it's in his genes." The purpose of this lie is to instill hopelessness! The Bible, however, teaches that people can be delivered from the sin of homosexuality and transformed by the power of God. (See I Corinthians 6:9-11.)

Even if someone believed he was "born that way," we should remember that celibacy is a gift. For His own reasons, God calls some people to celibacy, as in the case of the apostle Paul. "But I would that all men were even as I myself. But every man hath his proper gift of God, one after this manner, and another after that" (I Corinthians 7:7). In some cases, God may call a person to this kind of set-apart consecration to Him, and this call could be interpreted on a subconscious level as an aversion to the opposite sex.

Satan tries to convince us that we cannot help becoming involved sexually. He tells homosexuals that they cannot change or control their desires and that they simply must indulge in this lifestyle. But the Bible's admonition to all unmarried people, whether they struggle with homosexual desires or heterosexual desires, is to abstain from sexual activity.

The truth is that, if necessary, each Christian can live a pure and celibate life with God's help. I lived that way for over twenty years. Paul wrote, "He that is unmarried careth for the things that belong to the Lord, how he may please the Lord" (I Corinthians 7:32). God has recently provided me with a wonderful mate, and I can see my life and ministry taking a different direction. But the point is, no one has to have a sexual life, heterosexual or homosexual. Sex is a gift to a man and a woman who have been joined in holy matrimony. Any other use of it—homosexual or heterosexual—is not the will of God and is sin.

When You Learn That He (or She) Is "Gay"

Following are some tips I have gleaned and that can help the loved one of someone who has announced his or her homosexuality.

First of all, be calm. Although it may seem as if God has lost control, He has not. Nothing takes God by surprise, and He knew about this problem long before you did. So do your best to remain calm. When you first learn that a loved one is homosexual, that is not the time to try to deal with your own feelings of insecurity and fear. Try to focus on what the loved one needs from you at this particular moment.

Count to ten, walk around the block, but do not vent the anger. Remember, whatever you are feeling is normal for *you*. Do not be critical of your feelings of anger and helplessness and wanting to strike out. You are experiencing a true loss and can expect to go through the usual stages of grief—shock and disbelief, denial, anger, pain, depression. Try to flow with it, accepting that it is okay and normal under the circumstances. You have just been dealt an awful blow. Be kind to yourself, loving, and forgiving.

It is also vital that you communicate acceptance and unconditional love to your loved one. (We are not talking about approval of this lifestyle but acceptance of your loved one as a *person*.) He needs the security of your love now more than ever. You may feel that this person is a total stranger—and indeed this strange new part of him that you never knew before *is* a stranger. But he is still your loved one. He needs you more than ever. Do not let him feel that you are rejecting him when he needs you the most.

Acceptance is not the same as approval. We accept the person, but we do not accept the sin of homosexuality. God hates the sin; it is an abomination to Him. But He always loves the sinner. He loves the homosexual. He loves the person. Someone asked me recently if this attitude was not somehow a contradiction. Since her husband was an alcoholic, I asked, "Do you stop loving the alcoholic because he is alcoholic?" "No," she replied. She loved the alcoholic, but she certainly hated the alcoholism. Likewise, we can love the homosexual while hating his homosexual conduct.

"But I get so mad at him," she cried, "I could wring his neck!"

"Anger's normal. Just try your best not to communicate that to him."

Next, do not preach and lecture. The person has already told himself anything you might tell him. He has already struggled and fought and had countless conversations inside his head. You cannot add anything new at this point. By the time you discover your loved one is homosexual, he has already lived through all the torments. He does not need harshness or lectures.

Give the person unconditional love. Overnight, your beloved husband or child has become a stranger to you, but he is still your husband or child. Love him unconditionally. Your love is vital at this point. Constantly call on Jesus for strength.

Later, after you have assured him of your love and support, and when you are calm, you can talk to him in love about your disapproval of his lifestyle. But do not beat him over the head with Bible verses and information. Gently, with love and compassion, let him know that homosexuality is a sin, a lifestyle that grieves God. Let him know that you love him and will support him, and that you will always be there for him. But you must let him know, too, that you cannot condone the sin. You cannot compromise your own values and what you know to be truth from the Word of God.

Give the homosexual hope! Hold out an alternative for him. Let him know that the love and power of Jesus Christ can redeem and recreate him. Connect with a local ex-gay ministry, such as Exodus International, that can provide some concrete resources for him such as a counseling hotline, a brochure, a tape.

Unfortunately, all of this is just the beginning. Once you learn the truth, once you have regained your composure and begun to look to Jesus for help, once you have communicated your love and support, once you have placed a spark of hope in the person's soul—then you face a long journey! You will need support also. The homosexual lifestyle is filled with change, instability, broken promises, and shattered hearts. You can provide a listening ear, a place of warmth, security, and wholesomeness that sin will never be able to offer your loved one. But you yourself must have a strong emotional support system. Confide in your pastor and perhaps in a close, trustworthy friend or two. Ask if there is a local Christian support group for spouses or parents of homosexuals. There is real support in learning that you are not alone in this. Satan's tool, as usual, is to isolate you, to make you feel you are the only one in the world going through this particular problem. But you are not alone! God is with you and for you. And He has provided you with a network support system somewhere. Seek it out and use it.

In those long, lonely nights when the anger, pain, and sorrow seem overwhelming, try not to take it personally. Try to look at the person's homosexuality as a cold fact. It is not something intended to hurt you. It is not a statement of your failure or your value. Homosexuality is a very complicated problem. There is no one single factor that causes it, but there are a whole array of contributing factors.

Parents, especially, are vulnerable at this point. They spend many long nights of tears, praying and asking God, "What did I do wrong? What could I have done differently?" They must give it all to God. Perhaps mistakes *were* made. But those mistakes alone did not create the condition. Moreover, since God knows everything—the beginning and the ending—then He knows in advance the mistakes we will make and He makes provision for them in advance. God works even our mistakes out for good! (Romans 8:28). We must cling to this promise.

One of the hard prayers we must pray is that if our loved one is hiding sin then his sin be revealed. It must be brought out of darkness so he can repent. The homosexual confusion usually lies hidden in the person. Since God cannot allow sin into heaven, He allows it to come out now so that the person can be cleansed, healed, and made whole. As long as the person goes to church and everything looks all right on the surface, we would not know to pray about his problem. Once it is out in the open, we should thank God for His mercy in dealing with sin and ask Him for direction as to how to pray.

A song says, "Fight until you can't fight any longer. Then get up and fight some more." This is the theme song for those with a homosexual loved one. There will be times they feel like giving up. These are the times they must hang on with all their might. When we hang onto God, He will most certainly fight the battle for us.

We must stand still and see the salvation of the Lord! We must stand still and watch God work! He is still on the throne. He is still in control. The battle is not ours, but the Lord's. We must never quit praying. Sometimes we may cry out, "God, I've prayed for everything I can think of. There's nothing left to pray for!" That is when we start all over and keep praying. God will honor our prayers if we pray in faith. Sooner or later, we will receive assurance that He has heard and answered our prayer.

In the meantime, we must learn to praise, to be filled with thanksgiving. We must learn to delight ourselves in the Lord. He promises to give us the desires of our heart if we will delight ourselves in Him. Delighting in Him includes trusting Him. We must learn to leave our loved one in His hands, giving God the honor and the praise for still being in control.

Reactions of the Church

One of the hardest things the family member of a homosexual may have to bear is the reactions of friends, family, and the church itself. The subject of homosexuality often seems to bring out the worst in people. They experience fear, revulsion, and disgust. These are typical reactions, but they are also hurtful and emotional, and the church needs to overcome them. I know people right now who are sitting on the pews struggling with this problem. They feel they have no one to talk to about it, because they have witnessed these kinds of reactions when the subject was brought up in a group.

People make fun. They ridicule. There is no record, however, that Jesus laughed at anybody. The lepers—the outcasts of His day—He approached with love and healing.

We never know what might be going on in the heart of someone standing beside us. One youth, after he had left the church and drifted into the homosexual lifestyle, told me this story. He had been struggling for years with identity problems. His father had left him, and he longed for the strength and comfort of his father's love. In the midst of these struggles, he cried out to God for help and was seeking someone in the church he might be able to talk to.

He finally decided he would take a chance on the youth pastor. It was a windy afternoon youth outing.

Some in the group were walking along a levee when an obviously homosexual pair strolled by. My young friend stole a glance at the youth pastor, and as he did, he saw the pastor jab the boy walking beside him and sneer. My friend's heart broke as he watched the two of them begin to laugh and make ugly remarks. He knew right then he would not be able to make himself vulnerable to this pastor. Broken and confused, he ended up drifting away.

We must be compassionate! The pastor did not intentionally hurt this youth, but a thoughtless action turned out to be devastating. The Bible has much to say about idle words. We can talk about this subject and agree on what the Bible says about homosexuality. But we need to watch *how* we talk, because we never know who is watching us and what repercussions our speech might have.

A woman in the church had a son who had just gone into the "gay" lifestyle. I knew what she was going through, and so did the pastor. She had wisely decided not to reveal her burden to anyone else. We were working with her and knew God would help her through this problem. I watched her one day at a social. She was bravely trying to hold up, carrying her secret pain. Then one of the ladies brought up the subject of homosexuality, and the other sisters joined in. Before long, they were laughing and joking and making fun, and I watched my friend's face fall. She was crushed and I knew it. Oh, what pain and shame could be spared if we would watch our idle words!

Ministry to the Homosexual

In many cases, local churches have no ministry for the homosexual. A youth came to me and asked if I could refer him to someone who might help. I know a number of people who have been delivered from the homosexual lifestyle and are now serving God and doing a good job of it, but they are not willing to confess it.

If we can get past our personal feelings, we will see young people who are confused, lonely, and hurting. Many are in the stages of questioning, seeking, and looking for answers. If we cannot provide them, Satan will be sure to have someone come along peddling his lies, eager to deceive our young people. And we will lose them.

And then some will sit back and cluck and say, "I suspected it all along."

There are more Apostolic people than we realize who struggle with this issue. If we can reach them, and let them open up and talk about their fears and hurts, we may be able to rescue them. We need to reach them in time, to spare them untold agony and a soul lost through eternity.

There are also people who have already drifted into the lifestyle but who want to get out. They have tried it, and they have learned the hard way that things are much better in the church. But they are so deeply involved that they just do not know how to escape. I talked with one such young man. He really did touch me. "I don't blame anybody," he said. "I don't blame the church, and I don't blame Mom and Dad. I used to sit at that piano dying inside. I knew something was wrong inside of me, and I didn't know what. I began to read. I read a lot of stuff on being gay. And the more I read, the more it seemed to *fit*.

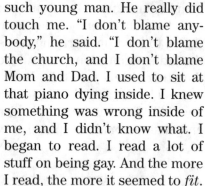

I used to sit at that piano dying inside. I knew something was wrong inside of me, and I didn't know what.

This was a nightmare, because I knew I couldn't go into that kind of thing. And yet, I didn't want to be alone all of my life. I would sit there, playing for the choir, and I'd be agonizing inside."

"Did you ever talk to a counselor?" I asked naively.

"I did. He's the one who pushed me over, because he

told me I needed to go ahead and get it out of my system, that I'd never have peace until I did."

I choked, "Why didn't you seek out a Christian counselor?"

"That *was* a Christian counselor." Both of us were at a loss for words now. After a minute, he went on. "I finally just gave up. And now I want out. It's bad out here, it really is."

"Why don't you come back?"

His eyes glistened with unshed tears. I saw his pain; it was all over him. "I don't know how. I don't feel any hope anywhere. I don't know how to get out of this thing; it's like a spiral. I just don't know how to get out of it. If I just had someone—a true Apostolic—who had been in this and then got out—if I could just talk to someone like that. . . ."

I have learned since that day that there *are* men who have been delivered and are willing to step out and talk about it. Some are part of Friends in Crisis, a Bible-based support group that meets at the Upper Room Apostolic Church in New Port Richey, Florida, where the pastor is Mark T. Huba. This group deals with all the hurts discussed in this book.

A man named David says, "Almost two years ago God did a marvelous thing. He delivered me from the homosexual lifestyle after fifteen long years. Friends in Crisis has been a real haven of help and healing. Being able to deal with all the hurt and pain and learning how to grow and let God have control has been a true blessing."

Bob, who has now been in church for two years, also has an awesome testimony, taken from the Friends in Crisis promotional packet. Bob wrote: "When I first came to Friends in Crisis ten months ago I was having strong feelings of suicide. I needed help! I had tried everything else: doctors, hospitals, prescription drugs, etc. At Friends in Crisis I found the love and caring I really needed. I have begun to deal with many hurts and issues from my past, which is making me a better person. I have peace and joy I never had before, which comes from my being saved through Jesus Christ, being baptized and receiving the Holy Ghost.

"At the age of six I was institutionalized until I was eighteen. While in the institution I was molested on two separate occasions. From this came a lot of fear and lack of trust of people. At eighteen I was released and sent out into the world. I was confused, not knowing how to function in everyday life and just plain lost. Then into my life came a man whom I felt rescued me. This ultimately brought me into the homosexual lifestyle. I led this life for twenty long years. I knew deep inside that I wasn't happy and that this lifestyle was wrong. I believed it was my only way to survive, plus I knew no way out! Healing over my molestation and homosexuality has been very painful. The first step was acknowledging the problems. Then came the hardest part—the forgiving of those who had hurt me. Many tears, much sharing, and of course praying have transpired. Through it all, I can say I have been delivered of my homosexuality! If you knew me ten months ago until now, you would have seen how through God and Friends in Crisis I have found that inner peace I was always looking for. Praise God!"

God loves them far too much to let them remain in a destructive lifestyle.

It is true that not all homosexuals want to be helped. But a growing number do. It is our job, mandated by the Lord Jesus, to take the gospel to them. We must give them the message that Christ forgives and is a God of love, compassion, and understanding. Homosexuality is not the unpardonable sin. God can and will forgive it. He will not turn away anyone who comes to Him with a tender and repentant heart. It is our job to tell this to homosexuals and to tell it in a loving and compassionate way.

Satan tells them that since God is a God of love, He accepts them just as they are. Otherwise, say they, it could not be said that He loves them. We need to communicate the message that God does loves them as they are, but He loves them far too much to let them remain in a destructive lifestyle. He has a far better plan for them!

But for the grace of God, there go I.

Chapter 10

Post-Abortion Healing

Thirty-two years ago, I had an abortion. Deep down, I really did not want it. But I did not think of it as murder. The majority of women who are suffering from post-abortion pain do not realize that the abortion in their past is causing so many problems. They have all kinds of symptoms—compulsiveness, depression, anxiety—yet are unable to see the correlation between the abortion and their present pain.

Have you had an abortion? God is a gentleman, and the wisest of all. He alone knows our seasons of healing. He will not ask us to seek healing before it is our season. He takes us through steps, one thing at a time. When it is time for your post-abortion healing, He will let you know.

Sometimes, He may call us to be healed yet we choose to remain in denial. We may say, "That abortion is over; I've been healed." Maybe that is true. And then again, maybe it is not.

Jenny knew something was wrong. She was not in denial. She just did not know what to do about it. Could you, perhaps, like countless others, be suffering from post-abortion syndrome and not know it?

What is post-abortion syndrome? We hear a lot these days about different kinds of syndromes. "Post" means "after." A "syndrome," according to the *American Heritage Dictionary*, is "a group of symptoms that collectively indicate or characterize a disease, a psychological disor-der, or another abnormal condition." A second definition is "a complex group of symptoms indicating a . . . dis-tinctive or characteristic pattern of behavior."

Lorrie Lenaghen is director of Wings of Love ministry, a post-abortion support group based in the Upper Room Apostolic Church in New Port Richey, Florida, where Mark Huba is pastor. She sheds some light on the mean-ing of this term: "It derives its theoretical roots from the post-traumatic stress disorder syndrome suffered by men returning from a bloody war, chiefly Vietnam. There are many elements of P.T.S.D., but several issues were isolat-ed, and these bring a clear idea as to the effects on sol-diers involved in the war. A chief issue was our inability to know who the enemy was—it could be a woman or child as well as a soldier laying out booby traps, land mines, fir-ing weapons, etc. This resulted in not being able to dis-tinguish the innocent from the guilty, as in our American naivete we assumed fighting would be soldier to soldier. Many soldiers returned home to jeers instead of cheers, and this added further to the confusion.

"Rather than talking about their experiences, many stuffed the horrors of war into the back regions of their minds and never dealt with their negative, destructive feelings. For many, life returned to simple day-by-day liv-ing. For others, eventually P.T.S.D. caught up with them. Some of the symptoms they feel are anxiety, suicidal thoughts, regret, guilt, sadness, inability to sustain inti-mate relationships, and feelings of loss, and they often resort to drugs, alcohol, and isolation to cope. It is well known that many homeless men fit this description.

"Women who have gone through abortion experi-ences mirror the same symptoms and behaviors. This is how post-abortion syndrome became identified."

These kinds of things are very real. You may have a cluster of symptoms that are wreaking havoc in your life.

You may even come to think of them as "normal." You may assume, without really thinking about it, that all people feel this way and live this way. So why try to change? You are in denial. But the day will come, if you seek the Lord and want to be the best you can be for Him and for His cause, that He will tell you it is time.

You will feel the gentle nudging of the Holy Spirit. Welcome it. If you do not feel ready, that is okay, too. As you read these stories of abortion, allow yourself to be open to any leading of the Spirit. Only God knows. Only God can do the work. He wants you to be whole and healed. He needs you for His kingdom work.

Ninety percent of illegal abortions were performed by skilled doctors, and the man who performed mine was a highly reputable physician. I was in a safe and sterile office. But a few hours later, I was holding a little "non-person fetus" in my hand. He had fingers and toes and a complete little male body, and—I have learned since then—a heart that had been beating and a brain that had been functioning. I have also learned that my little son could feel pain and that he had suffered horribly.

When I turned and walked away from that abortion, I buried it deep within me. There had been no problems, no complications, so I expected that was the end of it. Actually, it was only the beginning. But I could not know that then.

Abortion involves willful destruction of our very own flesh-and-blood offspring.

The aftermath of abortion can cause many things to go wrong in a person's life, things that often border on the insane. The reason is that abortion involves willful destruction of our very own flesh-and-blood offspring. It is the physical severing of a bond that can never be severed emotionally or spiritually.

Post-abortion syndrome is very real. It can create all kinds of problems, such as drug abuse and other destructive behaviors. But the good news is, there is healing. Some have read my story in *Goodbye, Granny Dix*. For those who have not, here is how God healed me. Healing can be yours!

My Healing

My own healing process started when I held my first grandchild in my arms. This little grandson was flesh of my flesh, and the sudden realization swept over me that God creates all relationships. His perfect plan for our lives fits together like pieces of a puzzle, and when we willfully destroy one of those pieces, nothing ever fits quite right. Something is wrong, but we cannot quite put our finger on it. When I looked into the precious little face of my grandson, I began to realize the enormity of what I had done so many years ago.

The next thing happened during a regular Sunday morning church service. I sat in the congregation worshiping God when I happened to glance up on the platform. As music director, my son Joseph was in his usual place at the organ. At his elbow stood another young man I had never seen before. He was a tall, handsome, godly-looking young man in his early twenties, probably a preacher. Although I did not recognize him, something about him looked strangely familiar.

Then his eyes met mine, and the Holy Spirit spoke to my heart. I knew that this vision represented the little son I had aborted those long years ago. His eyes did not hold hatred, only concern for me; and just as suddenly as he had appeared, he disappeared! Floodgates opened and I began to weep. God was there, holding me tight, and I wept through the remainder of the service. Weeping is not unusual in a Pentecostal service, and no one disturbed me. The brothers and sisters around me just allowed me the luxury of tears, but I could feel their prayers. They were being very sensitive to the Holy Spirit.

I wept for days after that. I realized I was going through something but I did not know what, because at that time I did not know the first thing about counseling women who had had abortions. I wrote a letter to my pastor, confessing my abortion. I wrote because writing is easier for me, but also because I did not want to put him on the spot of feeling he had to *do* something. I just wanted to make him aware that I was going through some kind of grieving process so he could pray for me. Prayer is so important!

I continued to let God have His way. Tears cleanse and heal, and I allowed them to flow freely during every service. Like Job of old, I worshiped. The key to the mystery of healing is worship—while we have our eyes and minds on Jesus and off ourselves, He can do wonders with the inside of us! In the midst of our darkest suffering, we should lift our hands and worship our Lord.

The pathway I found to healing was by tears; confession that led to repentance; worship; putting myself into the loving hands of God; submitting totally to Him, letting Him do this work in my life and in the secret rooms of my heart; and finally, reaching out to others with my testimony.

If you are part of a Spirit-filled congregation, you are already on your way. If not, look for such a church. Join in the services. Sing, clap your hands, worship, and praise. Ask God to give you the same healing and wholeness He gave to me, and expect it. Accept it when it comes. And thank Him with your whole heart. There is a new life ahead for you, beyond your wildest dreams. I know. I have found it.

Tabatha's Story

Tabatha is another sister who has found wholeness in Jesus Christ. Here is her story:

"I thought that this was an easy decision to make—

after all, it would only take a few minutes and my problems would be over! I had no idea how devastating the results of my decision would be.

"I was attending church sporadically, and I began to ask people there for advice. I needed to know what God felt about abortion. I asked them if it was in the Bible or if it would be wrong to have an abortion, and no one—not one single person I spoke to—told me it was wrong! They could not, or would not, show me in the Bible where it was wrong and a sin against God's Word. I was unlearned in the Scriptures, so I did not know. I actually thought it would be God's will for my life.

"After the abortion was over, I thought I would be happy. But instead I became so depressed that I wanted to kill myself. The fifteen minutes of counseling [so-called] I received at the clinic had not prepared me for this at all. I did plan on killing myself, all along begging God to forgive me but thinking it was impossible for God to forgive someone who had murdered her child.

"I became very good at hiding the pain; you learn to wear a mask. The people I hung around with didn't know all the emotional upheaval I was going through. Inside, I was so unhappy and so far into sin that I couldn't see the light of day. Outside, I was happy, thinking that everything was going great!"

She was in denial. Again, let us look at the *American Heritage Dictionary's* psychological definition: "an unconscious defense mechanism characterized by refusal to acknowledge painful realities, thoughts, or feelings . . . the act of disowning or disavowing; repudiation."

Tabatha's last statement is typical of denial: "I was happy, thinking that everything was going great!" As her story continues, we find more symptoms of denial.

"My friend . . . asked me flat out if I had had an abortion. I told her yes and waited for the condemnation. She just looked at me and smiled. That surprised me. She said,

'You're not over it yet and you need to turn it over to God.' I told her, 'I am over it.' But I wasn't—not by a long shot."

One of the hardest things in being healed from an abortion is forgiving oneself. In my own case, I always wondered about my precious little child. Where did his little soul go? Along with Tabatha, I had always felt that I had given up the right to grieve. But God released both Tabatha and me, and the first steps of healing began. Tabatha's friend had had a miscarriage at six months. She told Tabatha, "You know, I can just see our babies in heaven, playing and waiting for us to get there, and Jesus is taking care of them."

> *One of the hardest things in being healed from an abortion is forgiving oneself.*

After God releases us to forgive and be forgiven, we must also release our little child to Him. We must place our baby in the arms of Jesus and leave everything in His care. There is such peace in that! Many times I have had to do this, just as I must continue to do it today with my children who are grown. My children are in their thirties now, and in my mind I sometimes have to put them in a beautifully wrapped gift box and hand them to Jesus.

And then leave them there!

Lorrie's Story

Lorrie tells us: "What are my crimes? Five babies . . . I destroyed five babies. I know the world describes them as nameless, unidentifiable fetuses, but I know they were my babies. For years I carried the pain of my sin. Like a silent stalker, a terminal cancer, these actions caused my soul to remain scarred and comatose in spite of God's love and forgiveness.

"I went to a ladies retreat to find peace, and instead

the Lord informed me that He intended for me to deal with my abortions. There were no loud voices, no clanging, chiming bells—just a feeling that it was time now to be healed. I knew that what was happening was not just for me but for many other women existing in private, painful guilt galleries.

"Post-abortion syndrome does not always affect a woman immediately. Often it strikes when least expected or gradually engulfs a life without notice. A trigger, some significant event, sound, smell, or person transmits the memory, which in turn signals a return to the abortion experience."

Failure to bond with future children is also a symptom. Lorrie continues: "I began to pull away from them, fearing that if I got too close they would be taken away from me. I built a wall of protection for myself by denying the natural bonding that should occur with a mother and her children. I now know that this is a real condition known as post-abortion syndrome, which is an interruption of the bonding process with future or present children due to an abortion experience.

"Healing requires an open heart to God, a willingness to let go of our fearful past. I believed the verse of Scripture that says if we confess our sins to each other we can be healed (James 5:16). But I so wanted to be accepted, and I was terribly afraid of my friends' rejection if I confessed my sin of abortion. Yet I knew I had to get past my feelings and to the real issue. My friends wept with me and listened for two hours as I disgorged my horrible past. We prayed together, and as we did, a beautiful, warm sensation filled my body, soul and spirit. I truly feel that God began the beautiful process of healing at that moment of confession."

Thank God for His wonderful provision. Thank God for His forgiveness and love.

Chapter 11

~

Loneliness

"I watch, and am as a sparrow alone upon the housetop" (Psalm 102:7).

Time magazine reported in 1977 that according to health studies single people are much more susceptible to sickness than married people. The death rate from heart disease alone is five times as high among widows between twenty-five and thirty-four as it is among married women of the same age. And the divorced of all ages are twice as susceptible to strokes as are the married.

Loneliness is a feeling of not being able to reach out to another person or having any other person reach out to us. It is a feeling of being isolated even in a crowd of people.

Many people attempt suicide out of sheer loneliness. One young person did great things in the church. She was a gifted singer, musician, speaker, and leader of other youth. Nevertheless, she felt as if she never quite measured up to what she thought she could be or should be. She was always striving to do more, accomplish more, be better. She was a perfectionist who tried very hard to win the love and approval of others. No matter how well she did, it was never good enough. This attitude resulted in a crippling feeling of loneliness. She attempted suicide but was able to go into counseling later. God was able to lead her out of this feeling, and now she is living a productive life, but also one that is fulfilled.

Christian psychologist Norman Wright in *An Answer to Loneliness* quoted a lonely woman who said, "I hurt deep down in the pit of my stomach; my arms and my shoulders ache to be held tight . . . to be told that I am really loved for what I am." Dr. Wright said, "Deep within each of us is the hunger for contact, acceptance, belonging, intimate exchange, responsiveness, support, love, and the touch of tenderness. We experience loneliness because these hungers are not always fed."

The married wife whose husband fails to understand her feels incredible loneliness. So does the child whose parents are too busy to spend time with him. The mother of toddlers feels loneliness because she has deep needs for fellowship that cannot be met through a child.

I have ministered in many nursing homes over the years. Loneliness has been the number one problem in all of them. The residents are nearing the end of their lives. Most of their friends have passed away or are dying right before their eyes. They are haunted by innumerable fears, and no one can seem to understand them. When I worked at Tupelo Children's Mansion, we would minister at two nursing homes every Sunday morning. The old folks loved having us come and preach, sing, and testify. They loved hearing the Word of God. But the thing they enjoyed the most was having the Mansion children come in and sing. The children, who were learning to reach out and to minister at a very early age, would go from room to room and pray and sing with these dear ones. They learned to touch the wrinkled old flesh and pray for the blessings of God upon them. The old eyes would light up, the sparkle would return, and the lines would crinkle up in joy. The breath of fresh youth, the tender touch of a child, would ease the loneliness as nothing else could.

The experience also ministered to the children them-selves. Service to others is one of the best ways to over-come loneliness. As these children reached out to help the elderly and to meet their needs, they learned a vital les-son: ministering to others is the best way to be ministered to. In meeting the needs of others, we will meet many needs of our own. Our own pains and inadequacies are swallowed up in service to another human being.

The Agony of Rejection

Over and over I run into grown people, people in their sixties and seventies, who still suffer from early rejection. Rejection is a big problem these days, and many are struggling to overcome its long-reaching effects.

Tricia talks about her struggles: "I had an alcoholic father who used a lot of verbal and physical abuse. My mother died when I was twelve years old and left eight young children. I then opened my heart to a spirit of inse-curity, not realizing it until adulthood. I always felt reject-ed and belittled by everyone, but I always remembered the times of prayer and family devotion with my mother. I was left to raise my seven siblings and determined not to become what people said or planned for me to be, because of the conditions we had to live in.

"Through marriage I thought I had found security, not realizing I was faced with another insecure person who had an addiction to drugs and other things. Three years later I received the Holy Ghost and learned that God can do anything but fail. I went through very hard trials dur-ing the duration of my husband's addictions. At times I got very weak and had to fight a spirit of suicide, but God brought me through and gave me the comfort and peace I needed. His Word was all I had, and continual praying was all I could do.

"God put me on a fourteen-day fast. This time was

extremely difficult in many ways, including an accident and hospitalization. My husband pleaded with me to break the fast, but as I looked at him I knew I could not. I was believing God for his deliverance and salvation.

"With God's help I made it through the fourteen days of fasting and prayer. After a few weeks my husband decided to go to the drug support ministry meetings with a made-up mind and a desire to be delivered. One year later my dad was delivered from alcohol, baptized in Jesus' name, and filled with the Holy Ghost. He became my prayer partner and friend. God brought us close together, and we both asked each other for forgiveness. God healed a lot of the hurt between my father and me. Three years later, he died.

"Two years after my husband's deliverance, disaster hit again. I was faced with something that happened thirteen years ago in my marriage. It really tore me apart emotionally, physically, and mentally. The pain actually felt as if someone had pierced me in my gut with a sword and kept twisting it. The devil thought he had won this battle. He thought this was his big chance to wipe me out. For years I had problems with some of my family members but did not know why. The more I reached out, the more I was neglected and turned away.

The pain actually felt as if someone had pierced me in my gut with a sword and kept twisting it.

"My husband and I went to our pastor for counseling. Bitterness began to set in, but God knows how much we can bear. I repented many times for unforgiveness, but the wound was so great. At times I hated my husband, but I knew I had to pray even more. Unforgiveness is sin, and God does not hear our requests with this in our hearts. Today I can say that God is a miracle worker. He is healing those wounds. God is teaching me how to love my husband through Him. He is making me whole. Since God has brought that darkness to the light, the tension and anger are not there any more. God is healing those old wounds, and we are learning how to trust each other again. All this came by prayer, because I know I could not do anything without Him. My will had to be broken so that God's will could be done. Through this God has allowed me to communicate with other women to encourage them. If He can use a donkey to speak, He can use me to do His will. I will continue to trust Him.

"For I, Tricia, am persuaded that neither death, life, angels, principalities, powers, things present, things to come, height, depth, nor any other creature shall be able to separate me, Tricia, from the love of God." (See Romans 8:38-39.)

From the Word of God, we know what God's response to Tricia is: *I love you, Tricia! Can you see, can you realize how much healing has been accomplished in your heart? I will never leave you or forsake you; no creature shall ever separate Me from you. You are in My heart, My child, and I love you with an everlasting love.*

If I am having trouble with loneliness, I should ask myself what the real cause is. Is it a communication problem? Feelings of inadequacy? Fear of being hurt? If loneliness is the result of circumstances, there is much in this book about "circumstances" that will give guidance and direction. Perhaps we need to follow a necessary grieving process. People grieve at different rates and in different ways. We must not allow our own grief needs to be dictated by what someone else feels is "normal." What is "normal" for one person may not be "normal" for someone else.

Sometimes we must be the one to reach out to others for friendship. If we move into a new area and the church already seems to have its own little groups, we can be extremely lonely. But we must purpose in our heart to make a concerted effort to reach out and show ourselves friendly. We must ask God to open doors of opportunity for us. If the pastor announces a need, we should be the first in line to volunteer.

These days few people seem to be willing to make commitments. Relationships are typically built on the possibility that people will not get along and may part ways down the road. Several states are implementing a choice now in marriage licenses. In Louisiana, for example, a couple can get either a "covenant marriage" or the usual marriage that can easily be ended by divorce. Lack of commitment is one of the leading causes of loneliness. A husband and wife can be extremely lonely sitting in the same room if they lack total commitment to one another.

Hebrews 10:25 says we should not forsake the assembling of ourselves together and even more so as the day approaches. God knows. He understands loneliness more than anyone. And God is the only one who can satisfy our loneliness. He created each one of us with a giant void inside, and only He can fill that void. He will never leave us or forsake us (Hebrews 13:5).

The Woman in Leadership

The called woman is a lonely woman. Loneliness is part of the lot for a leader, male or female. The higher one goes, the lonelier it gets. But, with few exceptions, it is lonelier for a woman than for a man. Men have each other. The woman usually stands alone.

Too many people make leadership a competition, but women should not try to compete with men. There is so much work to do that there is plenty to go around for everybody. The main thing, as T. F. Tenney says, is to keep the main thing the main thing. And the main thing is make sure our spirit stays sweet and our attitude right. The woman leader should not put on boxing gloves, but stay feminine.

If you are a woman God has called to leadership, He did so knowing you were a woman. You do not have to act like a man. Enjoy your work. Enjoy your femininity. Enjoy the company of other women leaders. Get involved in a network; do not hesitate to pick up the phone and call somebody when you need to.

Let go and let God work. Let Him have His way. Allow the Lord to work, to use whomsoever He will. He alone knows who is best equipped for a particular job. Do not quench the Spirit. Have revival by letting God move freely without getting in His way. Stay close to God. Take all your complaints to Him.

Death

Christy Taylor from Tupelo Children's Mansion spoke at a general conference about the time her mother died. Christy had made her a castle at school for Mother's Day, but she never had a chance to give it to her. She told how her mother died just before she arrived with the castle and had never seen it. Christy was so hurt. She has suffered so much loneliness. She still has the castle.

A friend in California lost her son to the dreaded AIDS virus. Through no fault of his own, he had received the tainted blood in a transfusion. She could not understand why God had allowed this to happen. She had cared for her son in his final months, and she missed him dreadfully. She would walk through the empty house almost feeling his presence. Her loneliness was inconsolable.

Margaret lost her husband, Billy. Sometimes she would get on his motorcycle and go riding off into the night, just because she felt closer to him on his bike. Irene lost her precious Odell. Now she was uprooted, selling one house, moving into another. Both Irene and Margaret had been married for years. They suffered the pain of widowhood, the pain of separation, the loneliness. Where there had once been two, now there was one. The "other half" had been ripped away. The gaping hole left there was hard to bear. But they have a God who loves them and who waits in the shadows, ready to comfort them, longing to love them and hold them close to His bosom.

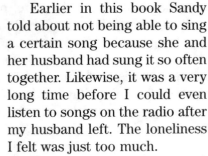

Loneliness.
It is a hole
created inside of
us, a void that
can only be filled
by a holy and
loving God.

Earlier in this book Sandy told about not being able to sing a certain song because she and her husband had sung it so often together. Likewise, it was a very long time before I could even listen to songs on the radio after my husband left. The loneliness I felt was just too much.

Paul's wife divorced him, taking their two children. He would lie awake night after night, wondering where they were and how they were doing. He said he felt as if his heart had been ripped out.

Loneliness. It is a hole created inside of us, a void that can only be filled by a holy and loving God.

God Understands Loneliness

If anyone can understand loneliness, God can. He longed for fellowship with Adam and Eve in the Garden of Eden in the cool of the day. How He must have suffered when He lost that fellowship!

When God came to earth in flesh, were things any better? Christ's disciples were rough fishermen who would certainly have rattled *my* sensitivities! In so many ways, they had an utter lack of understanding, and the lack of understanding makes for such a lonely feeling. When I am not understood, I feel very much alone. Jesus traveled this earth alone, and He died alone. He had to suffer in the flesh everything we suffer, and that included loneliness.

In Matthew 27:46, He cried out from the cross, "My God, my God, why hast thou forsaken me?" He echoed Psalm 22:1: "My God, my God, why has thou forsaken me? Why art thou so far from helping me, and from the words of my roaring?" The Spirit of God did not literally forsake the man Christ Jesus. Rather, His words and His cry express the abject loneliness of our Lord. Jesus Christ—God come in flesh—was spared none of the suffering. His cry was from the heart of a man who felt alienation! Of course, He gave Himself willingly. He laid His life down. At no point was Jesus ever at the mercy of anyone else—and especially Satan.

I have always been an independent lady, not requiring a whole lot of companionship. That is why, when serving in New Orleans some time ago, I found it rather odd that I was struggling so much with loneliness. I was busy in the work of God, sometimes sixteen hours a day, and I thoroughly enjoyed the work. I was surrounded by friends who meant a lot to me and deeply involved in the heartbeat of two churches. "So why," I would ask God in the middle of the night, "am I feeling this way? What's wrong with me?"

Soon I found the loneliness so deep and so dark that I began to pray a new prayer: "Lord, send me a husband." I believe that God led me into the loneliness so that He could answer this prayer. After more than twenty-two years of singleness, God brought me that husband, and I could not ask for a kinder, more understanding—or more *patient*!—husband. God knows what we need!

In the deepness of our darkest night, God is always there for us. A friend wrote me: "I've never struggled with loneliness the way I am now. We're here in a foreign country. I don't know anybody. There are no other people here of like precious faith. I feel such loneliness!" She went on to mention the book called *Hinds' Feed on High Places*. She told me, "When Much-Afraid starts on her journey to the Kingdom of Love, the Shepherd gives her two guides that will be her companions for the journey. She is horror-struck when she sees them, for they are Sorrow and Suffering. She is forced to hold on to the hands of Sorrow and Suffering as she journeys.

"As I thought about this the other day," she went on, "I thought about my own walk with the Lord and the 'teachers' and companions that He has asked to walk with me. They have often changed. Here, in the Azores, Jesus has asked me to take the hand of Loneliness while He directs my steps higher into His kingdom. I never thought about it that way before! So, in prayer, I said, 'Yes, Lord,' and accepted the loneliness as part of His plan for me at this time. I have felt much better spiritually, though my emotions and feelings still feel the same as before. It's not easy to accept unpleasant things, but at times it is needful.

"I have great comfort, though, for even at my loneliest, I *never* feel alone. It has brought me into a closer communion with my Lord that I had not thought possible. I have felt close to the Lord since I was saved, but not like this. So I am thankful for the lessons that I am learning and the Teacher who is teaching me!"

In those times, we, too, can experience His presence more than ever. We can spend much time in His Word, hearing His voice speak to us through its pages. As we read, pray, and commune with Him, a warmth and a glow seem to envelop us. And the night is sweet.

Because of *Him*.

Chapter 12

I Am the Abuser!

"Love suffers long and is kind; love does not envy; love does not parade itself, is not puffed up; does not behave rudely, does not seek its own, is not provoked, thinks no evil; does not rejoice in iniquity, but rejoices in the truth; bears all things, believes all things, hopes all things, endures all things" (I Corinthians 13:4-7, NKJV).

I remember the scene well. I was about eight years old, and my heart was about to beat out of my chest. I was so frightened I was in tears. And yet I instinctively knew I must be quiet. Shh! Very quiet! I sneaked into the dining room, just off the living room. That's where the phone was. And my brother-in-law was in the living room with my sister. He was drunk again, yelling obscenities at the top of his lungs. His language was awful, and I felt each word as if it slapped me in the face. He had just been released from jail for having almost killed her. Now was he ever mad and determined to fix her!

He towered over her. She was sobbing, begging him not to hit her. My heart, already broken in two, was racing. What could I do? I moved over to the telephone and lifted the receiver. I held the button down with my finger.

I stood poised to dial the operator. If he hit her one time, I would call the police! I was terrified, brokenhearted, in fear for my precious sister's life. Violence did something awful to my young heart. It touches everyone concerned and most of all the one being abused.

Robert

Years later, my position as social worker with an alternative sentencing program required that I go to the jail to interview a man named Robert. I needed to determine the extent of his problem to see if there might be alternatives to prison in his case. I did not want to go. I had already made up my mind that he was guilty, and I did not particularly care about coming face to face with him.

I had sat through his preliminary hearing and heard his wife testify. He had started beating her in their kitchen. She managed to escape to a friend's house a few blocks away. Robert stalked her. She told of the years of being beaten and verbally abused by this man. He was not an alcoholic; he just lost his temper. He said he could not control it when she "did her thing," as he called it.

"It's her fault," he told the judge. "If she would just stop that incessant talking! Always bellyaching!" Typical, I thought that day in the courtroom, always blaming the victim.

I made my way to the little room reserved for lawyers and their clients. Here I sat face to face with the inmate, nothing between him and me but a tiny little table upon which to take my notes. In the deep belly of the ten-story building, we were surrounded by the smells of the jail, the clanking sounds of metal doors, and the voice droning over the PA system. The rest of the world seemed so far away as I sat with this abuser, all alone.

I asked him why he abused his wife and was surprised at his answer: "I don't know."

That seemed like an honest enough answer, but I was

not impressed. He knew where I was from and that I could possibly get him a lighter sentence. I knew these guys—they would tell me anything—and sound so convincing! Again, my mind closed to him.

But sometime during the interview, I felt the Holy Ghost and knew that this man was telling the truth. He related how he had been beaten and abused as a child by his father and by an uncle. His mother would lock him in the tiny bedroom closet for days on end.

I did not want to believe him, but the witness of the Holy Ghost was so strong: *Get him help.* I did not think he deserved help—but then, I am not God. The upshot of the matter was this: the victim grew up to become the victimizer. The abused became the abuser.

Janice

I had known Janice for several years and thought I knew her pretty well. Now she sat before me, her face ashen, her eyes constricted to small pinpoints. "I've got to talk to somebody," she said, barely audible. And she began to weave a story to me that at first I thought she was making up. I could understand why she was ashen. It was a story of awful abuse upon her little body when she was just a child. She was beaten by a stepfather on a regular basis. For several years this abuse went on, and the anger built up in Janice. She would flail her tiny fists at him in pitiful attempts to hit him back and fight him off. He would grab her by the wrists, throw her down, slap her again, and yank her hair by the roots.

My stomach churned as I listened. Janice was even now a tiny five feet tall and cute as a button. It made me sick to think of her being hurt this way.

After she finished her account, she was dry-eyed.

"Janice, why did you come to see me?"

Her eyes dropped to the floor and then a tear came. It was followed by a sea of them, accompanied by gulping sobs. Finally, she was able to talk again. "Because, I hit Adella last night." Adella was her two-year-old daughter. "I mean, I abused her."

"I hit Adella last night." Adella was her two-year-old daughter. "I mean, I abused her."

"What do you mean, abused her?"

"I just lost it; I got so mad at her. She's in the terrible twos!"

I repeated, "What do you mean, abused her? What did you hit her with?"

"My fists. Over and over I hit her with my fists."

I tried not to flinch. Here it was yet again. The abused became the abuser.

Are You the Abuser?

Can you relate to these stories of previous abuse in your own life? Or are you still living in the shadows of memories that you have made to replace the bad ones, memories that you have shoved to the back shelves of your mind?

The abused and the abuser have much in common. One of these things is the long-forgotten memories. As the abused, the victim, you learned to live in a world of your own making, a world where the abuse was not taking place. You learned, like your victim now, to shut out the ugly, to disassociate yourself from what was happening. Or to determine that you would put it all behind you, never to remember it again. And you might also have determined never—never!—to hurt anyone else the way you yourself were hurt! And yet . . . here you are hurting . . . just as you were hurt.

Why is that? Why are you doing just what you swore you would never do? Why does the abused become the abuser? These are difficult questions, and I cannot begin to answer them all in this brief chapter. But if we can get enough understanding of the dynamics involved that we will allow the power of God to begin to work in our wounded lives, then it will be worth it. This one thing I know: God loves souls! And abusers have souls.

Statistics reveal that better than ninety-seven percent of parents who batter their children were battered as children. Janice grew up to abuse her own little girl. She remembers the hurt of being beaten, yet she does the same thing. She is aware of how much it is hurting Adella. "I don't want to hurt Adella!" Janice cried. "And yet I'm doing it! I promised myself I'd never do anything to hurt anybody else like I was hurt. Why?"

One reason is learned behavior. Another is the persistent attack of evil spirits. Another is the feeling of power, of control. Children who live in fear of never knowing when the next abuse will come, learn that they are powerless. They have no control over their lives or their own bodies. They grow up to feel this same lack of control as adults. They are small, inferior beings, children still, only now encased in grown-up bodies. Somehow, in some way, they need to get some semblance of control over their own lives. That most abusers drift into addictive lifestyles only compounds the problem. Whether they are overeating, drinking, or doing drugs, they lose control anew each time they promise they will quit and then do not.

Straight Talk to the Abuser

If you are an abuser, you need to be ministered to. Let us talk straight with each other. Hear me out. I understand some things about you, and that makes you nervous. But give me a chance. No one else will know. This is very private. Just you and me. And God.

The reason I know some of the things going on inside of you is because God has given me some knowledge and understanding. He has also placed a love for you in my heart. Really now—why would He do *that*? you may ask. Because He loves you. God loves you enough to accept you just as you are—but He also loves you too much to allow you to remain in this destructive lifestyle. He wants to minister healing to you. You see, Mr. Abuser, you are both a victim and an abuser. You need a double portion of God's healing. Can you accept this? *Will* you accept this?

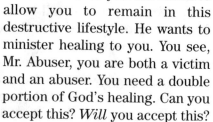

You are both a victim and an abuser. You need a double portion of God's healing.

You will not like to hear these words. But if you will get away in a quiet corner somewhere, all by yourself, just you and these words, and read them . . . God will meet you in that corner. He will be there for you. All I ask is that you not toss this book aside in violent denial. Give us a chance.

You are caught in a web of bondage. You are in bondage to a devilish, vicious cycle. You were attracted to the one you are abusing, just as she was attracted to you. You see, it is almost as if a victim wears a large magnetic sign saying, "Abuse me." An abuser can read this sign, whereas no one else can even see that it is there.

In addition to that, there are usually spirits involved in these dynamics, spirits that attached themselves to the abused and the abuser during the acts of abuse. Those spirits have remained with you all these years. When you pass a victim on the street, the spirit with you recognizes instantly the spirit that is with your victim. The spirits spot each other and are attracted to each other. The same is true of homosexual spirits. An acquaintance is struck up. It happens this way. You know it, and I know it.

The behavior you learned as a child is how you now relate to others more helpless than yourself—even though you always promised you would never hurt anyone the way you were hurt. You promised that, and you have broken that promise. And you feel guilty. You feel guilty because—let's talk straight with each other here—you have sinned. Unconfessed sin leads to shame. Shame leads to fear. And fear leads to a hard heart.

If we continue to live with sins and guilt that are unconfessed and unrepented of, we continually have to harden our hearts. Soon the heart becomes so hard that even we ourselves cannot reach into it. But God can! God can reach into the hardest of hearts!

God understands you when no one else can, not even you yourself. This does not mean that He approves of your behavior or will tolerate it forever. But He understands. As a man, Christ was tempted in every way we are, yet without sin. To be tempted is not sin. It is when we give in to temptation that it becomes sin. It is not a sin to be tempted to violence. Only when we do it, does it become sin.

So God understands what makes you tick.

He knows how it feels to be abused. After all, He suffered under the hands of the Romans and gave His life on the cross. He understands that you feel so small, so insignificant inside, that you tear up others just to feel superior to someone—anyone! He also understands that you know how to manipulate the very ones He sends to help you. They become the "authority figure" in your life, and you set yourself up to be abused by them. Of course it is not fair to them. And of course they do not understand it. You have, in essence, abused them, too, these helpers who are trying to care for you. They care for your soul. You place demands on them that they cannot fulfill. You put pressures on them that they refuse to bend to, and they end up feeling guilty because they fall into the trap that you set. With the guilt come more thwarted attempts to help, to the point that eventually the helpers become ineffective. It is seemingly one more victory for you!

But you are the loser yet again, and you will continue to be the loser as long as you choose to remain in your bondage. You see, when you run off those who can really help you, you then experience another kind of pain, that of separation, because you have separated yourself from what is positive and good. You also set yourself up for rejection again. It is a compulsive behavior with you. But that, too, can be changed under the power of God.

The power of God can do anything. The power of God is in me, and the power of God is in anyone who is filled with the Holy Spirit. You must receive a revelation of that truth. Ask God to help you grasp it. There is a spot somewhere inside you that God is able to reach if you will let Him.

Straight Talk to the Helper

There was a certain rich man. . . . And there was a certain beggar named Lazarus, which was laid at his gate, full of sores. . . . And it came to pass that the beggar died. . . . The rich man died also (Luke 16:19-25).

Helpers, those who have been sent by God to help an abuser, can only show God's love to this person by loving him! We must allow the love of God to flow through us to him. We have to see this person through the very eyes of God! How can we do this?

First, we need to recognize that we, like the rich man in the preceding Bible story, have had someone laid at our gate. If we can understand that God has brought us in contact with this abusive person for a purpose, the rest will come easier. The rich man probably intended to do something someday to help the poor beggar. But he never did; they both died first. We must not let this happen to us.

Sometimes dealing with an abuser is the hardest situation a leader or counselor will face. Frequently, the victim is a saint in the church who has an unsaved husband. Our first concern is for the saint. But God has laid her abuser at our gate. If it takes spending a week on our knees, we must allow God to bring us to the place where we have genuine love for this man. He will sense, otherwise, that our attitude is just a put-on, and he will retreat into his shell even further.

Abusers are very difficult to deal with, because they exercise so much control through their abuse. They need to be ministered too, first of all, as a prior victim. We must encourage them to allow God to heal their own childhood abuse. The story of Sister Lorene, told in the chapter entitled "Wives Who Hurt," has a happy ending. Her husband was won to the Lord by some brothers in the church who prayed, fasted, and allowed the Lord to work through them. Today he and his entire family are serving God. He is a leader in the church and a lay minister.

The brothers are so thankful today that they hung in there. They felt like throwing up their hands in frustration so many times. They would cry to each other that there was no hope for this man. But the power of God can do anything, and the power of God was in them. The power of God is in everyone who has been filled with the Holy Spirit.

Chapter 13

Anger and Rage

"Be ye angry and sin not: let not the sun go down upon your wrath: neither give place to the devil" (Ephesians 4:26-32).

It is time now to take a look at anger. Is it sin? How can we handle it? What, exactly, are we talking about when we talk about anger?

Anger can range from icy hate to boiling rage. Anger should be one of our best understood, most carefully managed, and most effectively channeled emotions. It is much too powerful to be overlooked, much too dangerous to be ignored. As we begin to look at how to resolve anger, we have to admit that anger, in and of itself, is not sin. Anger is an emotion, and like all emotions, neither right nor wrong. It is what we do with anger that eventually receives such a label.

Ephesians confirms this concept when it instructs to be angry and sin not. Some counselors have failed to help their patients with the problem of anger because they do not accept that anger is a normal emotion. But God gave us the ability to feel anger. Therefore, we must realize that there are constructive, God-called uses for it.

Our emotions are not destructive in themselves,

because our emotional makeup is from God. He gave us the capacity to live richly and fully, spanning the gamut of emotions. However, our emotions can become destructive when we fail to express them in harmony with biblical standards.

A sister in the church told me that for many years she had not been able to forgive her husband for some things he had done. She would have violent temper outbursts but, when asked, she said she did not have a clue as to why. Then God began to deal with her and to explain to her that all this anger was directed at her husband. "But, Lord," she argued, "I've forgiven him. I just don't think about it."

And so the Lord proceeded to explain things to her. I asked her how she finally overcame the anger. How was she able to forgive? She said simply, "I did it at the altar. All the time, every time there was a service, I'd go to the altar and do business with God. And finally one day, it just came. It swept over me like a warm glove! It was gone. He took it away!"

But often things hurt so much that we shut Him out along with everyone else.

I can think of no better place to "do business" than at the altar. God has the answer to every need, every pain, every worry. But often things hurt so much that we shut Him out along with everyone else.

When we are in the throes of anger, though, or any other strong emotion, that is the time we need to go to God and ask, "Why, Lord?"

A Personal Experience with Anger

I had never quite experienced traffic like this. Drivers in New Orleans were just as nerve-wracking as those on the Champs-Elysées—and they nearly terrified me to death back in my youthful days!

146

I was out and about in New Orleans a lot, zipping around on hospital visitation, Bible studies, counseling appointments. For the most part, I had been able to go with the flow, so to speak. The day came, however, when I found myself becoming nervous and angry. Drivers would push up to my bumper; lie on the horn; zoom through red lights, missing me by mere inches; curse me; and glare at me. The incessant horn blowing was enough to give even Job a nervous breakdown!

Each day that I ventured out into this combat zone, the anger mounted. Soon the anger turned into fear and hurt as I found myself pulling over on the shoulder and dissolving in tears. I could not understand this. "What," I cried out to God, "is happening to me?"

I began to feel terribly vulnerable. It was almost like being abused by other drivers. I realized it was not something personal on their part. They were the same way with other drivers, not just me. So why the feeling of being violated and abused? It did not make sense; I knew I was being irrational.

One night in service, I sat there a bundle of nerves. I had just come through the combat zone and was filled with anger. I knew the altar service would soon begin, and I would be expected to minister in the altar. And yet I knew I had nothing to give! I was depleted! "Dear God," I cried, "what is happening? Why are You letting me go through this?"

Suddenly, in answer to that prayer, my understanding was opened. The anger I was experiencing was because of past abuse that I had buried deep. I began to have flashbacks there in the congregation—flashbacks of being a child, abused, and so helpless! That feeling of helplessness at the hands of the abuser turned into anger. Anger turned into hatred for the abuser. Helplessness brought anger, tears, frustration. The same thing was happening in the traffic. God was allowing it so I could be healed.

I began to weep, because I had thought all the memories were behind me. I thought all the healing had taken place. Yet there I was, in the throes of another flashback, feeling more helplessness, more hurt, more anger. I knew in my heart that there was nothing anybody could do for me at that point. This was a wound just being opened, and it was not the season yet for healing. There had been times when I had laid hands on a person and told her to receive her healing. And I had seen it happen, not because of me but because it was God's time.

But there had also been times when it had not happened. It depends upon where a person is in the healing process. I have come to recognize that certain look as women turn and leave the altar to go back to their seats. They have a hopeless, vacant look, a look of throwing in the towel. They have tried it again and still are not healed. Those are such frustrating times for me, times I long to hold them in my arms and make them be healed! But it is all in God's hands and in His timing.

I began to cry out to the Lord anew. "What, Lord, is the answer? How can I help others when I don't even have the answers for myself? Lord, whatever I have to go through, please teach me so I can help others."

I meant this prayer with all my heart. I share this testimony now to help others understand some things they may be going through.

Uses of Anger

An angry person should look inside himself and examine his heart. David Augsburger explained: "When you feel anger mounting, ask, What is my demand? How am I demanding change? What do I really want? An honest answer is like a dash of cold water. . . . In anger, one gets a rare chance to see the self sharply, unretouched. Look and learn. Your anger may be an index to your degree of self-love and self-conceit. Or it may be an unconscious admission of guilt. Guilt that needs to be confessed, forgiven, released. For example, anger is common to those with bad consciences or repressed guilt. A thief is far more angry to be accused of theft than is an honest man. It's more often the adulterer than the faithful spouse who flies into a rage when an affair is revealed. Anger can be far more revealing than even your conscience's warning signals" (Augsburger, 1988).

In the case of the New Orleans traffic, my "demand" was control over my own person. I wanted to escape from the feeling of helplessness. My anger was my way of saying, "Get out of my space! Give me room to breathe!"

Suppressing versus Repressing

We should not vent anger hastily. When we do, we unload our anger upon another person, aiming our destructive energies at someone else. We have heard many times the old prescription about counting to ten when we are angry. That is a good prescription. Sometimes the desirable thing is to suppress the anger. That gives the necessary time for *reaction* to become *response*.

Suppressing is not the same as repression. To suppress anger is to hold it in abeyance until it can be dealt with in a healthy and rational manner. Repressing anger, on the other hand, is to deny the emotion with such force that it is stuffed down into the unconscious. The person then proceeds to "forget" about it on a conscious level. Remaining very much alive, however, it continues to grow and fester until it must once again surface in another form, usually bitterness and resentment. The dilemma we face is how to dispose of the normal anger energies in a normal and constructive way.

Jay Adams tells about two kinds of people: the *problem-oriented* and the *solution-oriented:* "Christians who are problem-oriented tend to talk about the problem, feel sorry for themselves, start up blame-shifting operations, and focus their energies upon who is at fault. Solution-oriented Christians size up the problem, try to fix responsibilities, and then *turn as quickly as possible* toward solving the problem biblically. In the process, often they find it necessary to rebuke, but when they do so, they are able to rebuke *in love.* The rebuke, though anger-motivated, will be done for a loving purpose and *in a loving manner.* The energies of the emotion will be *focused* upon the *solution* to the problem, *not* upon the problem maker" (Adams, 1973, 354).

Jesus Teaches on Handling Anger

We should deal with anger according to Matthew 18:15-19. Jesus taught, "If thy brother shall trespass against thee, go and tell him his fault between thee and him alone: if he shall hear thee, thou hast gained thy brother." What Jesus spoke of was confrontation. The wronged person goes alone to the one who has offended him. He should not take the problem to various people in the workplace or at church. Usually this action, taken in love, is successful, and the relationship is restored.

But what if the brother does not listen? Jesus continued with instructions for handling the problem. In each case the solution involves some kind of loving confrontation. It does not involve repressing and hiding our heads in the proverbial sand in hopes the problem will go away.

The energies of anger are wasted and used damagingly when they are directed solely toward oneself or another. Under control, anger is to be released within oneself and toward others only in ways that motivate one to confront others in a biblical manner in order to solve problems. Anger is a powerful emotion, but its power to motivate must be used, not abused. This motivating power is used properly when it drives one to begin to rectify any wrong situation between brethren as quickly as possible. It is used biblically when it impels one to become reconciled to his brother immediately.

"Speaking the Truth in Love" (Ephesians 4:15)

It is crucial when confronting another person to do so in love. There are different ways of speaking the truth, but Ephesians 4:15 exhorts us to speak the truth in love.

I was in a boss-employee relationship once, and both of us were under tremendous amounts of pressure. Over time misunderstandings began to arise, misunderstandings that at first he and I both attempted to deal with and resolve. But somehow, with time, this process broke down and it became so much easier (on the surface, at least) just to let things slide. I remember thinking, Why bother? He doesn't understand, and it's just the same thing over and over, anyway.

At the same time, he was also feeling the same way, so we allowed the communication process to break down. I would try to deal with my emotions alone by pulling myself up by the proverbial bootstraps and forging ahead. What I was doing, however, was burying, or repressing, my feelings. In other words, my emotional factory was slowly clogging up and heading for an eventual shutdown.

The first thing we tried to do was speak in love, but not the truth. In other words, we would both deny to the other that we were angry, or upset, or hurt. We did not want to hurt the other and thought that denying the feeling would resolve the situation.

Next, he began to speak the truth, but to do away with the love altogether. He began to express his anger toward me and the helplessness he felt, but he spoke the truth without love. I would react to this and began to speak the truth right back. Without love. It is an easy thing to see with hindsight that this was contrary to the scriptural injunction and was doomed for failure.

His next move was passive-aggressive. He would get

at me in little ways, such as giving some of my responsibilities to others without a word to me. When I tried to confront the issue, it came out all wrong. I was on the defensive. We would walk away from each other wounded and smarting, determined not to have it happen again. Inevitably, it would. The relationship rolled downhill like a giant snowball. Today it is still wrecked.

Another case involved someone I will call Jill. Jill felt a similar thing happening with her roommate, Carla. Jill and Carla had been friends since high school, and both had gone on to marry. Jill's husband took a lawless path and was incarcerated in state prison. Carla was divorced. Both childless and compatible in so many ways, they resumed their close friendship and decided to take a house together.

Jill was a spotless housekeeper. Carla was not. The first time Carla left the sink filled with dirty dishes, Jill bristled but immediately took her feelings in check and did the dishes. The second time this happened, she did the dishes and again kept her feelings in check. She knew Carla was still hurting from the divorce and did not want to add to her pain by confronting her about this situation.

The next time it happened, Jill left the dishes piled in the sink, determined to leave them there until Carla took care of them. Carla did not appear to notice there was a problem, and every time Jill came into the kitchen she bristled all over again. On the second evening, they sat down together at the coffee bar. Jill immediately put up her wall so that her friend would not see her wounded feelings. Carla spotted the wall. "What's the matter?" she asked.

"Nothing. Why?"

Carla frowned. "You seem distant, almost cold."

Jill longed to get it off her chest but did not want to hurt her friend. "Nah, it's your imagination."

"You sure?"

"I'm sure."

But the wall remained, and it grew taller and wider in order to keep out the torrent of emotions that were building up. The inevitable blow-up happened, and Jill and Carla split company. It is sad and such a needless shame to see a friendship end like this. Had Jill followed the biblical injunction to speak the truth in love, it might have gone something like this:

Carla: "You seem distant, almost cold."

Jill: "You know what, Carla? You're right. There is something bugging me. And I see that I'm building a wall between us. I value you and our friendship too much to let that happen."

"What is it?"

"You know, I really can't function too well unless there is order in my life. I know everybody's not like that. But if things are a mess around me, I feel like a mess. You know what I mean?"

"Yeah, I think I do. But messes don't usually bother me. Have I left a mess that upsets you?"

Jill nodded toward the sink. "Those."

Carla smiled. "Is that all?" She sprang from the barstool and dug into the dirtied dishes. "I'll take care of it in a jif."

Such a different outcome!

Relieved, Jill would then join her friend, and together they would have the kitchen sparkling in no time. And Carla would try to be careful from then on. When she did slip up, Jill would not bristle. She would have more understanding and patience, because she would know Carla really was trying. The result would have been different because Jill took the time to speak the truth in love. Doing so is much better than silently stuffing our anger!

Jill could also have spoken the truth but not in love. She could have yelled and flown off the handle. The end result would have been the same as not saying anything. The Bible way is to confront the problem, to speak the truth in love, and to forgive.

(The preceding information on speaking the truth in love was excerpted and adapted from my book *Lord, Why Am I Crying?*)

Study in Proverbs

The Book of Proverbs is chock full of good advice on what to do with anger. Let us look at some of that advice now.

Proverbs 15:1, 18. The greatest contributing factor to anger is the mouth! Grievous words stir up anger, but soft responses will nip it in the bud. In Matthew 5:23-26, 38-42, Jesus taught us to resolve our differences through reconciliation and negotiation, not retaliation or getting even.

What causes a person to respond harshly? Pride—because he is on the defensive. A person may hide his real emotions behind a facade of so-called concern—but only for a while. The anger will, sooner or later, come out. When dealing with an angry person, we must be gentle. We must be determined to stay soft and humble. It is not the time to point out the other person's faults.

Proverbs 16:32. The ability to control ourselves—especially our anger—is of more importance than physical strength. If we cannot control our spirit, we open the door to the enemy. We become his prey, like a cat with a mouse. The conquest of *self* requires more true wisdom and more steady management than winning a war. A rational conquest is more honorable than a brutal one! When we conquer our spirit we are *more than conquerors!*

Proverbs 19:11. Do we have discretion? Deferring anger means having patience. If we are wise, we will control our emotions. Fools are controlled by their emotions. A wise person will ignore or forget the wrongs that others have done to him.

Proverbs 20:2. We need the favor of those in authority. Let us not offend them! It is foolish to provoke others to anger—even fathers are not to provoke their children to anger. Much more should we not provoke the King of kings to wrath!

Proverbs 21:14. If we offend someone, we need to go to that person privately. We must be humble and present a gift, if necessary. Who can stand before a humble person with a single flower in her hand?

The key word here is "secret." We should seek reconciliation privately, keeping the matter between the two people involved. We do not need an audience—nor the grapevine "praying"—for that could negate our very purpose!

Proverbs 22:24-25. A person who is living in sin will reap trouble and frustration. Such a person will often lash out at others in anger. Eventually he will be destroyed.

We learn from those with whom we associate. It is vital to keep company with Christians who are truly Christians. We do not want to learn the ways of an angry person! Anger is a snare to the soul. A mild-mannered person who runs with an angry one will also become an angry person in time. We must decide what kind of person we want to be and then have fellowship with that kind of person. It is the law of friendship that we try to be accommodating to our friend, ready to serve him or her.

Proverbs 25:23. The backbiter can tell from people's faces whether or not they want to hear his words. If we hear something evil spoken about our friends, we must show dislike—if not in word, then at least by our look. We must show ourselves uneasy. This can bring conviction. We must not sit silently while a good person is maligned.

Proverbs 29:22. An angry person will stir up strife by words or deeds. The strife will grow more intense. A furious person will not regard what is right. Sin will be his lifestyle. Undue anger is a sin and the cause of many other sins.

Chapter 14

When Faith Fails

"**A**ll rise!"

The judge came bounding up to the bench, his black robes flying. Court was in session.

Susan eyed him sharply. He seemed like a nice enough man. The hearing should not be too bad. She had entered the courtroom that morning, her faith in God at a peak she had never before known. She knew, beyond a shadow of doubt, that God was going to deliver her child that day. It had taken a long time to get to this place in faith and many long nights spent in brokenness, in weeping alone in the darkness. But God, as always, had pulled her through and had planted this faith in her heart. Now she thrilled to her new, unflappable faith!

A smile of contentment played around her lips as she sat quietly in the courtroom watching her son. He was at the long mahogany table at the front of the cavernous room, his attorney at his side. He was going to be called next, and she could tell he was very nervous.

But not her. Not Mama! Well—a little, maybe. She had a God who could take care of this problem. She was certain her son had learned his lesson and would never be involved in any kind of crime again. God had chastened him, so the worst was over. She had hired the very best attorney at great expense and sacrifice. She had spared nothing; she had insisted on the best for her son. She could not bear the thought of leaving her son's future in the hands of a public defender, so they had mortgaged their home to hire this man.

She settled back into her seat, the proceedings rumbling quietly in the background. Thoughts of her beloved son crossed her memory. The newborn baby. The boy off to first grade. Receiving the Holy Ghost. Living for God. Busy serving the Lord. Until . . .

Robbing a bank is a federal crime. "Oh, dear Lord," she cried inside her heart. How it does hurt to see your boy go wrong! Susan recalled now the many long and dark nights when she had cried all the tears she had. She had lain awake in the dark, wishing she could cry again and shed more tears. That was better than this awful dead feeling. And it was healing, the shedding of tears. But Susan had shed all she had. Dry sobs would often accompany her agony in the night, dry sobs dwindling off into pain that simply could find no expression.

But her God had come through for her again. He had filled her with beautiful, soaring faith. She had the certainty—that absolute *knowing*—that He was going to have her son walk out of the courtroom with her today.

No—this was too much! "Lord, what happened, where did You go?"

The judge banged the gavel; the show rolled on. There he stood, her handsome son! He had learned his lesson and was ready to return to the land of the living. The voices droned on, Susan barely aware of the proceedings until the gavel sounded again. What had happened, why was her son waving his arms around in devastation?

The bottom line for Susan was that things had not turned out as she had hoped. She had been so certain that God would come through for them. What went wrong?

As she watched her boy go through the doors one more time and disappear down the long hallway toward the holding room, she almost collapsed. No—this was too *much!* "Lord, what happened, where did You go?" Somehow she made it home, fell into bed, and pulled the covers over her head. She felt that God had failed her— or was it just that her faith was failing?

"My Children Are Divorcing!"

Helen could not believe what was happening. Divorce! In this family? No! We all live for God; we all love Him and serve Him with all our strength. We do not even believe in divorce. God puts families together to *stay* together! What, pray tell, is happening?

But the news was sure. Her daughter-in-law was divorcing her son and taking the children. Her grandchildren! Nobody ever talked about the pain that grandparents go through in a divorce. Helen was learning fast that this was the most horrible pain she had ever gone through: seeing those little babies ride off with their mama at the wheel, riding off into who knows where? All the hopes and plans for the children . . . watching them grow up in Sunday school . . . singing in children's presentations in front of the church . . . watching the little heads in the front pew, lifting their hands in worship and praise. What would happen to all that? What kind of chance do children have, being raised by a backslider? What kind of home will they live in? Will they get to go to church at all? Will they ever come to know who Jesus is?

"I loved this girl like a daughter," Helen cried, "and now I'm not even allowed to see her and the kids. This is like a death. Except, you know, it's even *worse* than death, because they're still *here*, still *alive!* I went through all the stages of grief—shock and disbelief, anger, fear, depression."

159

Jesus told Peter that He had prayed for him that his faith would not fail. What happens today, in the kind of world we are living in, when our faith fails? What comes next? What is after faith? How does one hold on to the promises of God when faith in those promises has gone?

Susan, after the long ordeal of watching her son leave for federal prison, discovered a new level with God. "When your faith seems to fail," God whispered in the night, "is when *trust* kicks in."

God never fails. He just takes us higher and higher. Even when it may seem that our faith fails, we can rest assured that He is working in us. Trust goes much deeper than having faith for a miracle. We must hang onto His dear hand with all our might and just keep walking.

Faith

We must look at faith very seriously, for Hebrews 11:6 tells us that without faith it is impossible to please God. To lack faith in God is to lack trust in Him. It is, in effect, calling God a liar. Those are strong words, but sometimes we need strong medicine. If we are to see miracles and conversions sweep the world, then we must have faith.

Having faith is really not difficult. We do not have to sit around working it up. Faith, like every good and perfect gift, comes from God. Faith is *built.* Faith *grows,* from one mountaintop to the next, from one miracle to the next. But we must simply, faithfully plod along in the circumstances God gives us on a daily basis.

Yes, God indeed gives us our circumstances because they are what we need to learn the lessons He has prepared for us. So instead of fussing and complaining about them—instead of letting them overwhelm us and beat us down—let us recognize them for what they are. They are items on His divine lesson plan, building blocks, nothing more, nothing less.

*And she said, As the L*ORD *thy God liveth, I have not a cake, but an handful of meal in a barrel, and a little oil in a cruse: and, behold, I am gathering two sticks, that I may go in and dress it for me and my son, that we may eat it, and die. And Elijah said unto her, Fear not; go and do as thou has said; but make me thereof a little cake first, and bring it unto me, and after make for thee and for thy son (I Kings 17:12-13).*

Never mind how Elijah must have felt, asking for food for himself first. Can you imagine how depressed this poor widow must have felt when she was out gathering sticks for their last meal? In spite of her personal feelings, however, she went about trying to fulfill her duties and responsibilities to home and her young son. Another meal must be prepared. The stress of her circumstances must have been staggering. She seemed to have no one who cared or would help. She had resigned herself to what appeared to be inevitable.

When we study this precious woman, we find no evidence of great and aggressive faith. So what caused God to include her in this great miracle? Close reading shows that this woman had enough faith ("as a grain of mustard seed," Matthew 17:20) to accept the Word of God and act on it. She manifested simple obedience. She did not understand. We are not told how, but according to verse 9, God had commanded her to feed the prophet. The confirmation came in verse 14, when Elijah told her, "For thus saith the LORD God of Israel, The barrel of meal shall not waste, neither shall the cruse of oil fail, until the day that the LORD sendeth rain upon the earth."

Her pure and simple obedience to the command of the Lord was effective. God wants us to trust Him so that in turn He can trust us and depend on us. More than anything else in this whole world, I want to please Jesus, and without faith it is impossible to please Him.

Stressful circumstances in life often furnish the stage and the script for the display of God's mighty power. This woman's willingness to simply accept and act on the Word of the Lord with unquestioning obedience turned promise into provision. What situation is God allowing in *our* lives at this very moment in which He might make His mighty power known?

Make yourself a prayer list. Remember to record *answers* on that list. Answers build faith, and new, more aggressive faith is nurtured by past promises fulfilled. We can live from glory to glory, for all power in heaven and earth belongs to our God!

Will God *Really* Provide Our Needs?

Have you ever watched a little child with his hand safely tucked in his parent's hand? He safely crosses the street, clinging to Daddy's hand. He feels safe and protected. He trusts his daddy.

That is how God wants us to be—safe and secure, with no reason for alarm, because we trust in Him and He is our heavenly Father. He will supply all our needs; all we have to do is trust and obey Him. Of course, faith requires that we take action, for faith without works is dead (James 2:17).

We must step out on faith. When we do, we have the promise of II Corinthians 9:8: "And God is able to make all grace abound toward you; that ye, always having all sufficiency in all things, may abound to every good work."

Remember when you learned to ride a bicycle? What happened the first time you fell off? Did you quit, give up? Or did you get back on and try again, falling again and again, until finally you could ride it everywhere?

Contentment

What is the secret to being content? The key lies in the kind of activities we spend our time doing. Since we entered this life with nothing, and it is guaranteed that we will take nothing out of it when we leave, the best thing we can do is to spend our time doing God's work.

The happiest Christians in the world are those who are working for Jesus, who are winning souls for Him. They are more content with fewer material possessions than those who live in abundance but do not make any effort to share the gospel. Those who work for Jesus are content and blessed of God.

We can be content serving God wherever His will leads us. Wherever God calls us to work in His kingdom, He will also give us grace to be happy and contented doing His work. In whatever we do, if we do it unto the Lord, we have the joy of the Lord. Hebrews 13:5 says, "Be content with such things as ye have." Because we are humans, it is not always easy to follow this advice, but it is the will of God for us to do so. It should be our goal as well.

Many people struggle with contentment. It was always a battle for me, because a part of me was always stretching, reaching for more from God and for His kingdom. The battle raged in me for years until Sister Nona Freeman taught me: "It's okay to be content but not satisfied." That made sense. It described how I felt. I am content with where I am but not satisfied to remain there forever.

The last words of Jesus as recorded in Matthew were, "Lo, I am with you alway, even unto the end of the world." What a promise! He has never broken that promise! Where He sends us, He will go with us. He will provide for our needs. No matter what circumstances come our way, we can be content because contentment is a result of choice. We can truly choose what kind of life we will lead and whether or not we will be happy or sad, contented or discontented.

"The LORD is my shepherd; I shall not want" (Psalm 23:1). There is no lack in Him. We are complete in Him. He is our protector, and He is our provider. As children bring their broken toys to Daddy, we can bring our broken dreams and our problems to Jesus. He will fix them!

When I was a single mother raising two children alone, circumstances tested my trust and faith over and over. Once while we lived in Tulsa, Oklahoma, God asked me to visit a lady in a home for alcoholics about seventy miles away. I had no gas in my car and no money to put gas in my car, and I had not been in Tulsa long enough to make the kind of friend I could ask for money. But the Lord said go, so what else could I do? I *could* stay home, I supposed, and tell myself surely I misunderstood God because He would not want a poor woman with two little children to be stranded out on the highway. The other choice was to jump in the car and go, trusting Him.

I went. We arrived safely. We did run out of gas, but only after we had safely arrived in the distant town. I met the alcoholic woman and ministered to her. God provided enough gas for us to get back to Tulsa through another person who needed ministering to in that little town. It made me think of the time our Lord said, "I must needs go through Samaria."

God never asks us to go anywhere that He does not go along. He is our protector!

God never asks us to do something that He is not along to help. He is our provider!

But sometimes I catch myself thinking, I'm not worthy. . . . If I can only pray harder . . . If I can only fast more . . . The centurion said he was not worthy, but Jesus healed his servant without ever seeing the servant. God wants to help us, just because He is God—not because we deserve it! Our blessings are predicated on our faith in God, not our goodness, or our spirituality, or the amount of time we pray. *He* is the Savior, not us!

Let us renew our commitment. Let us renew our trust and our faith. Let us renew our decision to trust Jesus.

When we step out on a limb, He will be at the very end of that limb, waiting for us.

Jesus Is the Fact Changer

Jesus is the fact changer. Even when the doctor says there is no hope, there is hope in Jesus.

A dying man is told there is nothing more that medical science can do. He learns to accept this so-called fact and allows it into his soul. The soul also becomes sick because of the same inoperable cancer; the person is now in need of *double* healing. The problem has become a *faith problem* in addition to a physical problem.

Proverbs 4:20-22 says, "My son, attend to my words; incline thine ear unto my sayings, Let them not depart from thine eyes; keep them in the midst of thine heart. For they are life unto those that find them, and health to all their flesh." Once we receive these words into our heart, we must hold onto them. They will begin to influence first our thinking, then our spirit, and then our body. Healing will result.

Trust

Trust in the LORD with all thine heart and lean not unto thine own understanding (Proverbs 3:5).

Susan in the beginning of this chapter had reached the place where she could not understand what was happening and she no longer seemed to have faith for the miraculous. At this point, trust would have to kick in. Trust means *resting* in God. Having done all, we must stand.

I have done all I can do for my son, Joseph. Sometimes it seemed that he was making his way back, and I would be so encouraged. My faith would soar! I would phone friends around the country to say, "He's on his way back;

please pray! Help him over this last hump!" And I would live in a state of expectancy, like Susan. Any minute now, I would hear the news that the prodigal son had come home! There is nothing quite like that kind of faith.

And then off he would go, back into something else. I would feel such frustration, hurt, and confusion. My faith would take such a nose-dive, and I would be so far down I had to look up to see bottom. "God," I'd cry into the night, "what has happened?"

Sometimes I would not hear from God. He would stand off in a corner somewhere in the shadows, watching me, seeing what I would do. I would turn to the right and to the left and could not find Him there. What darkness! "God," I would fumble around in the blackness, "where are You? Why did You leave me here alone? You promised, Lord!" I'd whine. "You promised never to leave me!"

When faith for the miraculous fails, trust must kick in. The Scriptures may look barren. The promises that once vibrated with hope may now seem so empty. Still, it is the Word of God. The Word of God is vitally important, because there will come a time when everything else will fail us.

When the world is crumbling into a million little pieces all around us, it seems difficult to have faith.

Trust in the Lord with all thine heart and lean not unto thine own understanding.

But trust is so hard!

That is because flesh has failed, not God. That is because there is nothing else that flesh can do. As long as we can do something, there is hope. But when prayer, fasting, and reading the Bible do not seem to work, and yet the world is crumbling into a million little pieces all around us, it seems difficult to have faith. The hurt is so deep, so penetrating, it feels as if it will break us.

Trust in the Lord with all thine heart and lean not unto thine own understanding.

"But, Lord, I need some understanding. If I have some understanding, then I can trust!"

Trust in the Lord with all thine heart and lean not unto thine own understanding.

"But, Lord—"

No buts. Just trust.

Let us open our mouths and speak it out. Even though the words may sound empty and hollow, let us speak them out. The angels will hear. The devil will hear and he will tremble. Jesus Christ is still Lord; Jesus Christ is still on the throne. Jesus Christ is still in control.

Trust in the Lord with all thine heart and lean not unto thine own understanding.

Chapter 15

Sexually Abused!

*"The spirit of the Lord G*OD* is upon me, because the L*ORD* has anointed me to preach good tidings unto the meek; he hath sent me to bind up the brokenhearted, to proclaim liberty to the captives, and the opening of the prison to them that are bound" (Isaiah 61:1).*

The physical wounds of abuse usually heal with time. What might have been a sliced piece of flesh will pass away in time and be forgotten. What will remain are the wounds to the soul. These rarely heal, apart from the Lord's help. Unless someone steps in with intercessory prayer and a heart full of compassion, these pains may never be healed, because the victims do not even know that healing is available to them.

They continue to suffer in the added pain of their isolation. Not only do they suffer, but so do those closest to them. Usually, it is all done under the cloak of something else. No one figures out what is going on, what the real problem is. How can they find a solution if they do not even know what the problem is?

According to Isaiah 61:1, Jesus is standing by, ready to heal those secret wounds, to heal those dear ones with hurts that no one else can see. But Jesus knows all about them.

Those who bear the wounds of sexual abuse often have a difficult time finding help. There are many dear men and women of God who are full of compassion and who stand ready to do the will of God, yet they will not touch these kinds of situations. They are not comfortable with them, and that is all right—if they are willing to point the suffering ones in the right direction to someone who *can* listen and help. I have heard pastors say, however, "She is *my* saint, and I will not refer her to any kind of counselor, biblical or otherwise. I'm protective of *my* people!"

All I can say in response is that I have seen this approach fail too many times. We are dealing with *God's* people. Undershepherds will be held accountable for people if they did not do all they could for them while they were in their care. Getting into the Word of God for healing and cleansing is never wrong. Jesus said His Word cleanses (John 15:3).

Becoming One Flesh

Paul wrote to the Corinthians, "What? know ye not that he which is joined to an harlot is one body? for two, saith he, shall be one flesh. . . . Flee fornication. [The Greek word is *pornea*, meaning sexual intercourse.] Every sin that a man doeth is without the body; but he that committeth fornication sinneth against his own body. . . . Glorify God in your body, and in your spirit, which are God's" (I Corinthians 6:16, 18, 20).

When a man and woman, or a boy and girl, are joined in sexual unity, they become one in flesh and spirit. Should they separate, their spirits are torn asunder, causing great emotional distress. (By the way, this teaching explains why we should be very careful about whom we marry. We should never marry someone whose spirit is not one we would choose for ourselves.)

Many of the troubles a victim of sexual abuse experiences stem from the prior spiritual attachment with the abuser. The abuser's sin affects her profoundly, and it is possible for her to grow up to become sexually immoral or abusive herself.

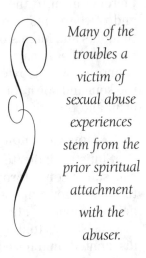

Many of the troubles a victim of sexual abuse experiences stem from the prior spiritual attachment with the abuser.

The story of Carrie Eastridge, *Shoutin' on the Hills,* provides an example of this principle. Her husband, Earl, was an inveterate adulterer. She became desperately ill and could not get well. One day she called in a weak voice for her daughter to bring a Bible and sit beside her. She said, "Sis, read I Corinthians 6:15-16."

Sis read: "Know ye not that your bodies are the members of Christ? Shall I then take the members of Christ, and make them the members of an harlot? God forbid. Know ye not that he which is joined to a harlot is one body? For two, saith he, shall be one flesh."

Sister Eastridge explained: "You see what Earl does, Sis? He'll be gone for two or three days, or weeks, then return very contrite. I know when he's saying 'never again' that it won't last a week. But because I love him so much, I'm his wife again. So I've been receiving his sin into my body. Now my life depends on my taking a stand. The very thought of it hurts unbearably; however, I have no choice."

When her husband returned she took her stand. She informed him that she would cook and clean and wash but not be his wife physically. This hurt her very much. But she told him that when he decided to be faithful again, they could be one again. And she was completely healed!

Hebrews 4:12 tells us, "For the word of God is quick, and powerful, and sharper than any twoedged sword; piercing even to the dividing asunder of soul and spirit, and of the joints and marrow, and is a discerner of the thoughts and intents of the heart." The Word of God alone can heal the damage done to the soul and spirit. Humans cannot know the extent of the wounds perpetrated upon the soul and spirit, but the Word of God is living and powerful and provides the answer.

How Common Is Childhood Sexual Abuse?

Statistics indicate that one out of every three females will suffer some form of sexual abuse during their lifetime. Stop for a moment and look around your church or neighborhood . . . one, two, three.

The stories told by survivors of sexual abuse are often discounted, minimized, or ignored. Such responses make victims feel more alone than ever. When we understand the dynamics of childhood sexual abuse and its ongoing effects on the victims, then we will be able to provide support and healing.

Child Protective Services of the Minnesota Department of Human Services reports that approximately eighty-five percent of the reported cases are committed by persons known to the child or her family. These are people who have power over children. They tend to be those closest to the child, such as parents, siblings, grandparents, baby-sitters, and teachers. The places where the child is supposed to be the safest are the very places where she is in greatest danger—home, school, church, library. Particularly the home. Many children cannot rest in the sanctity of their own little beds at night, not knowing when *he* will sneak in again, filled with his venomous deceit and pain!

Adult women survivors of childhood sexual abuse are all around us. They sit in the pews, teach Sunday school, sing in the choir, and preach in the pulpit. The best support leaders can offer is an open mind and heart and a willingness to listen. Even if there is nothing we can do to help, just by their having someone to believe them and listen to them will bring much healing.

What Is Child Sexual Abuse?

Because experiences of sexual abuse affect a survivor's ongoing emotional and spiritual health, it is helpful to know the full range of past abuse that may cause a woman's problems today. Sexual abuse is not confined to intercourse but may also include touching in a way that makes the child feel uncomfortable, showing pornographic materials, talking in a sexually explicit way, or any kind of photography or filming of a child in a sexual manner. Anything done to children that could cause them to feel guilty, ashamed, dirty, or uncomfortable could be abusive.

Helping Victims Escape Their Past

Pastors, leaders, and people who simply care, may sooner or later be called upon to help a person who has been abused. If you want to help someone, first and foremost, listen to her story. A survivor must be believed if she is to be healed. More than anything else, she needs someone to believe her. Listen kindly, and be very careful how you react. It does no good to react strongly and angrily.

On the other hand, do not show an overabundance of sympathy either. She does not need sympathy, for sympathy never helps anybody. What she needs is *empathy*, which means feeling as another person feels. How can you feel like that when you have never been abused? Maybe you have never been abused in that particular way, but probably there have been times when you have been betrayed or felt violated. Maybe you were robbed or burglarized.

Maybe a best friend betrayed a confidence. There is an experience somewhere that you can now draw upon. Those old feelings of being violated, abused, and soiled begin to come back. That is empathy. It will help you and the one you are listening to connect and relate. She will be so grateful!

Sometimes it is difficult to respond without hearing both sides of the story. If you have an idea that the abuser might be innocent, still be very careful to acknowledge the hurt of the woman. Never indicate that you think she is lying or exaggerating. You do not want to raise questions or fear in her; you want to get to the bottom of the matter. Having her retreat is not what you want. If she is telling the truth, she needs to be helped. So does the abuser. If she is not telling the truth, she still needs to be helped. In all probability, she will be telling you the truth, unless there are other factors involved. Sometimes people going through divorce and child custody battles can react in ways they would not otherwise.

The abused person needs to be reassured that the abuse was not her fault.

The abused person needs to be reassured that the abuse was not her fault. She needs to understand that she was the victim and that she did not do anything wrong. No one ever has a right to violate anyone else. In this regard, we need to watch our words. Some things we say, actually meant to help, might hurt. For example, we should not say, "It only happened one time." That does not matter. The pain is every bit as real. The act was every bit as wrong.

Another inappropriate statement is, "It happened so long ago." Again, when the abuse occurred does not matter. Saying things that put more guilt on the victim, such as moralizing and preaching at her, does not help either. She does not need to hear that. She has already told this to herself for a long, long time. She probably already knows everything you might say to her. She is trying to cope, she is trying to get on with her life, and she is trying to forgive. The only thing is, she is having a hard time doing these things.

One of my clients confronted her abusive father. At first he denied everything, saying it never happened, that she had only imagined it. Then he relented somewhat and admitted that, while it did happen, it was not as she remembered, it was not as bad as she thought it was. Finally, he said the magic words, "Oh, all right, I'm sorry!" But they did not ring true. They were sarcastic, and she sensed that he was only saying them to get her off his back.

The next day her pastor, meaning well, told her that she should just forget it now that he had said he was sorry. But she knew different. She knew that the pastor wished she would accept this so he could close his own file on it. She felt victimized all over again.

When she explained her feelings to her pastor, he made matters worse. He said, "He just made a mistake; we all make mistakes."

It is important to keep the process open-ended. It is our nature when solving problems to want closure. However, imposing our own timeline or expectations on the survivor can be counterproductive.

The Example of Tamar

Howbeit he would not hearken unto her voice: but, being stronger than she, forced her, and lay with her. Then Amnon hated her exceedingly (II Samuel 13:14-15).

Tamar trusted her half-brother Amnon and willingly did a good deed for him. She loved him and expressed that love by taking care of him when he was supposedly sick. Imagine her horror when he changed the order of business, when he betrayed her in the ultimate way. Not only was this an act of rape, it was also an act of incest.

Typical of rape victims everywhere, Tamar tried to talk her abuser out of doing this thing. She tried to reason with him. She appealed to his emotions, to his good name. Nothing worked, and he proceeded with the awful act. His own lust satisfied, he tossed her aside. Tamar felt this kind of betrayal was worse than the first. She was like a used doll, thrown out in the trash. Verse 19 tells us she "went on crying." It was not just a bout of crying, but it continued on and on.

Tamar mourned. She felt grief. People who are violated feel deep sorrow and grief. It is as if something has died, and what they refer to is the death of their emotions. Sometime during the abuse, they just shut down. They lose their self-respect, their identity, and all hope.

Tamar ended up spending the rest of her time in her brother Absalom's house—she "remained desolate." We do not know all the story, but Tamar apparently did not receive much empathy and support from her brothers and a do-nothing daddy. Absalom was so insensitive all he could say was, "Hold your peace, sister; don't take this to heart."

Without counseling and a strong support system, abused people are headed for a life of feeling shamed and inferior, humiliated and grieved. Typically, the abused never seem able to get free of the assumed guilt. They begin to feel that the shame will remain with them all of their lives. Tamar remained in her brother's house and probably became a morose and depressed person. Why did Absalom wait "two full years" to go after Amnon? Could it be he grew weary of having to deal with Tamar's broken spirit? An unhealed victim can be a difficult person. She is so full of hurt and pain, bitterness and unforgiveness.

There will be no healing without forgiveness. It is as vital to the process as air is to breathing. A whole chapter will be devoted to the subject later. Forgiveness may take different forms. For some it means finding personal peace. Others discover that the perpetrator, though disturbed, is a human being as well. Some survivors experience forgiveness only when they can forgive themselves and complete the healing.

Making Referrals

It is vital that, as Christians, we have knowledge about the referral process. We must be very careful when referring an already fragile personality. When we are in over our heads, we can damage the healing process. We can help the victim get to a counselor or therapist who specializes in sexual abuse. However, even after making the referral, we still have a responsibility to continue our love and support.

The local rape counseling center can be a good resource for referrals. It is a secular agency, supported in part by public funds, but it can be just what someone needs. When I was director of such an agency, we contracted with a counselor who specialized in sexual assault counseling. She would come in one day a week to work with victims. She did not go into things that were unrelated to the recent assault, because there was not enough time. (I called it "spot counseling," sort of like "spot reducing.") If they needed counseling in other areas, they were referred elsewhere. Several pastors allowed me to refer saints to her, and the women were able to find healing.

Many pastors have learned that Tupelo Children's Mansion is an excellent referral source. Here is a testimony from a child at the Mansion:

"My mother was eighteen when she had me. My father never stuck around. My mom then met this guy and they got married. He promised to take care of me as his own, but he left us.

"Mother met another man who was an old friend from elementary school. They began to date and eventually got married. At first he was an okay guy, but then he began to beat us so bad that we would hide in fear that 'Daddy' would come home drunk or high and beat us.

"I can remember when he would try to teach me to roll a joint at seven years old. 'Daddy' then began touching me and making me do things to him also. That went on for a while, and I told my mother one morning that 'Daddy' was making me do things that made me feel uncomfortable. She confronted him and he denied it. So we left town. He found us, admitted it was true, begged my mother for forgiveness, and she let him come back.

"One night I woke up and saw him trying to choke her to death! I made noise to distract him. Then I told my mother that he had again been molesting me. He ended up going to jail.

"By the time she married again, I had become cold to the father figure. My new 'daddy' and I never got along. He tried to take control of everything and pushed me off to the side. I would be grounded to my room for six months at a time. My grades fell drastically. I got depressed, then went on drugs. It got so bad that I ran away.

"Finally I went to live with my pastor and his wife, and things began to turn around for me. I got off drugs and gave my life back to God. I didn't have much of a family life there because we were always on the go and had only four or five sit-down meals a week. They wanted something better for me. So when we heard about Tupelo Children's Mansion, we filled out the application. Since I arrived here, I have received direction in my life. I have a lot of support from my new family!"

She is another life changed because of the Mansion— and also because of a wise pastor who cared enough and recognized the need to refer. She is in a place where she can receive the love and counseling she needs. She can now find healing for the hidden wounds that could twist and destroy the rest of her life.

Love covers a multitude of sins. God loves us. He understands, and He stands ready to heal.

If you are hurting, go to Him right now. Ask Him to bring into your life the kind of help that you require . . . the people . . . counselors . . . books . . . other resources. He knows you better than anyone else.

Chapter 16

Joy in Suffering

"Verily, verily, I say unto you, Except a corn of wheat fall into the ground and die, it abideth alone: but if it die, it bringeth forth much fruit" (John 12:24).

I was in the home of some ministers recently who have been valiantly struggling to raise up a work for Jesus. They gave up everything to go to a small town. In the corner of the living room was an old rocking chair. "See that chair?" the woman asked me, her eyes twinkling with joy. "I rocked all my babies in that chair."

I was impressed. (And maybe a little jealous, too, that someone could hang onto something for *that long*—I have moved around so much.) She told me, "When we came here, we had a big, three-bedroom house full of good stuff—now we're living in this basement in a church! I don't have much, sister," she said, her eyes sparkling with memories, "but my husband knows—where *we* go, this chair goes!"

Loss has always been one of the hardest things for me to accept. Like having to let go of my children. (Maybe I still am struggling with this!) But we only learn the true meaning of certain biblical principles as we travel through hard things like bereavement, pain, loss, frustration, disappointment, and heartbreak. Sorrow seems able to put into our hands a golden key that can unlock to us treasures of truth and new understanding. The following verses from Ecclesiastes 7 proclaim this truth:

- "It is better to go to the house of mourning than to go to the house of feasting."
- "Sorrow is better than laughter, for by the sadness of the countenance the heart is made better."
- "The heart of the wise is in the house of mourning."

Forsaking All for the Gospel

Verily I say unto you, There is no man that hath left house, or parents, or brethren, or wife, or children, for the kingdom of God's sake, who shall not receive manifold more in this present time, and in the world to come life everlasting (Luke 18:29-30).

When the Lord first began to deal with me about leaving my home in California, this passage of Scripture became the guiding one in my life. I had made California my home for twenty years. My children were there. My three grandsons were there—and now also a brand-new, two-week-old granddaughter, after we had given up hope of *ever* having a little girl! When she was born, I said, "Surely, Lord, You don't mean for me to leave *her!*" But God confirmed His Word with signs following, and so it came time to leave. He opened doors for me in Louisiana.

My home sold without advertising, for more than I would have asked for it. The new owner needed all my furniture and anything else I cared to leave. I loaded up my little station wagon with my few little treasures and left everything and everyone behind. It was just God, my cat, and me. God had done a quick work. My head still spins as I look back at how fast everything unfolded and fell right into place. Sometimes we have to wait inter-minably for God to move. We just know that He has lost our address, and the waiting can become most difficult. But He is ever busy behind the scenes, getting everybody ready, preparing hearts, putting everything in its place. And then, not too early and not too late, He moves! And things happen fast. That is the way it was when it was time for me to leave for a place I had never even visited.

I learned that it is one thing to consecrate at the feet of Jesus and another thing to follow through with that consecration. It is one thing to promise to go where He leads and another to actually walk away from everything we love. But God's grace was with me every mile of the way. And He provided C. B., the sweet little kitten with personality plus, to teach me about laughter and to place his little cheek against mine and dry my tears. What a loving, understanding God we have!

Although driving out of Los Angeles for the last time was a sorrowful thing, the joy I had was absolutely strengthening. I felt so close to God, I knew He was in the car with me! His presence was utterly breathtaking, and I had peace knowing that I was in the will of God. That is the joy of suffering.

"Most gladly therefore will I glory in my infirmities, that the power of Christ may rest upon me. Therefore I take pleasure in . . . distresses for Christ's sake: for when I am weak, then am I strong." I am no apostle Paul, but I can relate to what he said in II Corinthians 12:9-10. To have the power of Christ rest upon me makes it worth it all.

Learning Obedience

Though he were a Son, yet learned he obedience by the things which he suffered; and being made perfect, he became the author of eternal salvation unto all them that obey him (Hebrews 5:8-9).

One of the hardest lessons for most of us to learn is that God has His own way of working out His will in our lives. He has His own time. The foregoing passage of Scripture tells us that Jesus, the Son of God, learned obedience and was made perfect by the things He suffered.

Well, that was Jesus, we might say. And Jesus was God. That is not for *me!* But wait! We need to see what the Bible has to say about that. I Peter 2:21 tells us, "For even hereunto were ye called: because Christ also suffered for us, leaving us an example, that ye should follow his steps." Very clearly then, we are instructed to suffer as He suffered. We need to find out how.

Suffering is not our favorite topic. One reason we have such a difficult time with suffering is that we usually are able to see only one side of it. Jesus was reviled and persecuted. The suffering inflicted upon Him is our example. In the middle of our suffering, we should follow His steps, His example.

I Peter 2:21-23 speaks of Jesus' response. Whatever He did, we are to do; the way He responded, we are to respond. For instance, when Jesus was reviled, the Bible says, "He reviled not again." In other words, there was no such thing as revenge in our Lord's life. When He was threatened, He "threatened not." He just went right on doing the will of God.

The Word of God has much to say about pain and suffering, and we do not particularly care to hear about it. But suffering is inevitable; it will happen to all of us. Thus we need to study how to respond to it. Will we fight against it, hindering the work of God in our lives? Or will we submit to it, permitting God to mold and shape us by the very thing that hurts so deeply?

"That's all well and good," you say. "But you don't know what I'm going through."

No, I do not, but there is One who does, and He is the One who has given the instructions. Not only does He know what you are going through, and how deeply you hurt, but He Himself also suffered. He is ever close to those who suffer. This is "the fellowship of his sufferings" (Philippians 3:10).

I had not been in Louisiana very long at all until I was ready to take a trip back to see my children. When I threw my arms around them at the airport, it seemed like ages since I had last seen them and touched them. We enjoyed our visit, just being with each other, and all too soon it was time to head back. The last night of my visit, my son took his mother to an elegant restaurant. We enjoyed the evening very much. Over dinner I kept enjoying his fiery dark eyes, sparkling almost as though they were dancing by the candlelight. On the way out, I picked up a book of matches with the restaurant's name and logo on it.

On the flight home, I nestled in the little seat, holding the prized book of matches in my fingers, savoring the memory of Joseph's eyes when we were together. It was just a little something to remember him by. I could never forget my son, of course, but souvenirs are something special to most of us.

I had always thought it might have been nice if Jesus had taken an absolutely perfect body back with Him to heaven. Why did He keep the scars? Isaiah 49:15 says, "Yet I will not forget thee. Behold, I have graven thee upon the palms of my hands; thy walls are continually before me." Perhaps we can say they were His souvenirs—memories of time spent on earth with His precious children and the price He paid to redeem them. Just as I would not forget my son, neither would He forget us. Oh, how He loves us!

Led into the Wilderness

And Jesus being full of the Holy Ghost returned from Jordan, and was led by the Spirit into the wilderness (Luke 4:1).

Often we find ourselves in a wilderness. I have been there many times. There are always other places we would much rather be. When we are in our wilderness it is easy to get angry at the devil and rebuke him. We should not necessarily blame the devil for our wilderness experiences, however.

According to Luke 4:1, the Spirit led Jesus into the wilderness! There He was tempted by the devil. But the devil did not *put* Jesus there; he *met* Him there. Too many of us tend to blame the devil for everything—especially for things that cause suffering. But according to the Word of God, Jesus was led into the wilderness by the Spirit.

Reaction versus Response

Jesus *responded* to temptations and suffering rather than merely *reacting*. Our life can be transformed if we learn how to respond instead of react to the hurtful things in our lives. Reacting is like a mindless knee-jerk. Instead of grumbling and moaning, complaining and resisting, we can learn to think through our situation. Then we can respond on a higher, spiritual plane with praise, thanksgiving, and faith. If we live for God and have given God control of our lives, then we can rest in the knowledge that everything that comes into our lives has come with His permission. He has a good purpose for our lives and will work everything together for that purpose. When we are living for God and doing the best we can according to His will, then we can rest in the simple, childlike trust that He knows what He is doing.

When problems arise, we should search our heart to see if something is there that ought not to be. We should discuss our circumstances with the Lord. After doing so, if we still remain in our situation, we should stop fighting against circumstance but continue to trust in God. Let us learn not to resist what God is doing in our lives. If He allows sorrow and grief, we should not resist it but endure it and learn from it. A study of Exodus reveals that God does not approve of murmuring and complaining. Psalm 50:23 says, "Whoso offereth praise glorifieth me: and to him that ordereth his conversation aright will I shew the salvation of God."

"Stand still, and see the salvation of the LORD" (Exodus 14:13). In time of need, we are to look up into the face of God. Quietly and without fanfare, we should submit ourselves to Him. Then, with a whisper from our hearts, we thank Him and praise Him and worship Him. Job of old fell down and worshiped.

Reacting with praise and thanksgiving and joy releases power to bring good out of evil. Yes, we can thwart even the actions of our greatest enemy himself with praise and rejoicing! Out of Satan's plans and works, God can bring glorious victories when we react with praise to Him. Our praises actually become avenues on which God can travel to transform the evil into good, mourning into joy, and ashes into beauty.

Murmuring, on the other hand, sets up roadblocks. Complaining and depressed thinking interferes with God's work on our behalf. But in acceptance lies peace, as Amy Carmichael has said. In the willingness to let go (as He gives us strength to do it), by opening ourselves to receive what He has chosen for us, lies a joy that nothing else can give and a peace that nothing in the world can either give or take way. When we practice the two principles of praise and acceptance we become invulnerable to Satan's tactics. Nothing can harm us. Although some things can still bring us pain, with the pain will come healing and blessing.

These lessons have come long and hard for me. It has been so very difficult for me to learn to praise and respond with joy when my whole world was crashing down around me. And I am still learning. Yet the Lord demands that we trust in Him with all our hearts and lean not unto our own understanding. Several years ago, the Lord assured me that the way to see my children saved was for me to be happy and content. I heard Him loud and clear, but because my children were at the time saved and because habits of depression were so deeply ingrained in me, I could not really apply what God had said. I filed it away in my subconscious, and it has resurfaced again.

I have never felt that I deserved to be happy. Happiness was not fostered in the depressed household in which I grew up. I remember one time in particular when my mother looked at me through her tears. I had received a triumph at school and came flying home, happy, joyous, exulting. The response I got at home was, "But how can you be so happy when your mama is suffering, honey? Don't you care about me?"

This type of response was all she knew to do. She did not feel that I loved her if I was happy while she was hurting. I do not blame my mother; she loved me in the only way she knew.

But as I began to let the principle of happiness and contentment sink into my thinking, I began to realize that it produced a power in me and such startling and magnificent results as I had never before supposed possible. The more I practiced this principle, the more power it created. My whole body began to react differently. My ulcer went away, my blood pressure stabilized, and my energy level soared.

In conjunction with happiness and contentment, there is another important principle to practice; namely, surrender. We must not try to hold onto anything in this life, but we must willingly let it go in order to receive new enrichment from the Lord. "Except a corn of wheat fall into the ground and die, it abideth alone: but if it die, it bringeth forth much fruit" (John 12:24).

Everything that we willingly lay down at the feet of

Jesus bears in it the germ of resurrection life. Things that we refuse to lay down are finally forced from us and bear in themselves the seed of death. The worms of bitterness, resentment, and self-pity eat into the heart of them and destroy the seed of life. What is forced away from us is lost to us indeed, but what we willingly lay down into death will be raised to life again in the form of something even lovelier than what we laid down.

The home missionary wife mentioned at the beginning of this chapter is dedicated to God, and if God said she needed to give up her rocking chair, she would do so. But some people would not—or could not, because they have not yet come to the place in Christ that they are willing or able. Let us not have such a foolish attitude. I Corinthians 15:36 admonishes, "Thou fool, that which thou sowest is not quickened, except it die."

Let us give everything to Jesus! Even when we are on the mountain top, we should not try to hang onto that experience. Whatever we have, let us be willing to let go of it in order to receive the new joys and riches that the Lord has planned for us. If our arms are loaded down with dead wood, the Lord cannot fill them with something else. Bitterness, unbearable pain, sorrow, and loss lie in trying to hold onto the things we can no longer keep, in the refusal to let go willingly, in the desperate and frantic clinging to the objects we treasure, the idols of our hearts. We suffer intolerably in mind and often in body because of our passionate clinging to the familiar objects of our love that have so entwined themselves into our hearts that the thought of being severed from them is a torment and a horror.

Joni Eareckson Tada told about receiving a letter from a young woman who was legally blind. She and her husband wanted to know if Joni had a biblical answer to the question of whether it was right to bring children into the world when there was a possibility the child might inherit the handicap. Joni, after much searching of her Bible, gave Exodus 4 as her answer. When Moses felt that he could not speak to Pharaoh, God answered him in verse 11: "Who hath made man's mouth? or who maketh the dumb, or deaf, or the seeing, or the blind? have not I the LORD?"

God controls all things! Even genetic mistakes come under God's sovereign control. God knows our families before we are born, and He designs a plan for each of us in light of the circumstances of our birth and upbringing. God has a plan for us just as He did for Moses. That plan called for the cooperation of a mother who would dare to make a little basket and hide her child in the river. God has a plan for each of us and for our children.

God had a perfect plan for Jacob. Jacob was a tough one. His name meant supplanter, or deceiver. Jacob had a long way to go, but God got him there. None of Jacob's actions took God by surprise. He was destined to receive the blessing, even though Esau was the firstborn. At first glance, it would seem that God had made a mistake, but God knew what Jacob and his mother were going to do. He knew that the birthright would be stolen. Jacob lived as a fugitive in a foreign land for twenty-six years. He was repeatedly treated unfairly by his father-in-law. He was cheated out of the woman he loved and worked for for seven years. Then in later years, after he had won Rachel, he lost her to death. He suffered extreme grief, even to the point of having suicidal thoughts, after his beloved Joseph was presumed eaten up by wild animals. And yet God worked all these events together for ultimate good, for God knows the ending from the beginning.

Joseph went through many hardships. He was rejected by his brothers, sold into slavery, taken off to Egypt, and thrown into prison for fleeing from a woman's advances. It would have been easy for Joseph to have doubted God. Yet Joseph was in God's will throughout the whole process. He stated in Genesis 50:20, "But as for you, ye thought evil against me; but God meant it unto good." If Joseph had remained at his father's side, he would not have been able to deliver the whole family in time of famine. Jacob went through the deep heartbreak of losing his cherished son to what he thought was the jaws of a lion, yet in the end his son was restored to him.

Suffering creates brokenness in us. Until we are broken, we cannot be used as God plans. Even Job had to be broken so that his remaining 140 years might bring glory to God. Not only should we not reject suffering, we need to accept it when it comes and flow with it. Indeed, we should ask God to break our human will and pride by whatever means God deems necessary.

It is not risky to pray this kind of prayer. God knows where we are and what we can bear. He will not bring us through something too great for us to bear. If we can pray this prayer from the depths of our heart, it is because God has led us to do so and knows we are ready. He will go through the experiences of brokenness with us and will ensure that we are not overwhelmed.

I ministered in a small church a couple of years ago, and toward the end of my message I felt impressed to ask the people to come forth and pray for brokenness. It was scary to me. But one by one they came, and they cried out for God to break them. When I left this church, I worried that I had done the wrong thing. It seemed such a drastic step, and I worried that dire things might happen to those who asked to be broken. But two years later, they are in revival. The church has nearly doubled. All those who prayed for brokenness are still serving God, in a more intimate, vital way than ever before. It is not because of me or anything that I did, but because God knows what He is doing. As we shall discuss in the next chapter, being broken is absolutely necessary for God to use us as He wills.

Chapter 17

The Necessity of Brokenness

*"And, behold, a woman in the city . . . came . . .
and stood at his feet behind him weeping, and began
to wash his feet with tears, and did wipe them with
the hairs of her head, and kissed his feet, and anointed them with the ointment"* (Luke 7:37-38).

Jesus went into a Pharisee's house and sat down to eat.
A woman of the city, who was a sinner, went in also and
wept and anointed our Lord's feet. This woman had a lot
of courage. She did not allow fear or intimidation to prevent her from performing this act for Jesus. All she cared
about was Him!

What about us? Is that all we care about—Jesus? How
many times have we stood at the feet of Jesus weeping?
When was the last time we were broken in His presence?

When we reach the end of our ability, with nowhere
else to turn but Jesus, and surrender all to Him in worship, then we feel the grace of God enveloping us. In our
brokenness, we reach for His hand, and He leads us out
of trouble and deeper into His grace.

Jesus explained brokenness in a parable: "The hour is
come, that the Son of man should be glorified. Verily, verily, I say unto you, Except a corn of wheat fall into the

ground and die, it abideth alone: but if it die, it bringeth forth much fruit" (John 12:23-24).

Here Jesus described His action in dying so that we might be saved. He had to be broken in order to bring new life to us. By extension, we too must become broken if we want to minister effectively to a lost world. We cannot add anything to His atoning work, but when we die to the flesh and the world, we make it possible for God to work through us to reach sinners.

The flesh that the Bible talks so much about is not merely our physical bodies, but it is our carnal nature. *Webster's Dictionary* defines "flesh" in this sense as "human nature, especially in its sensual aspect; the carnal nature of humankind; sensual appetites."

There is a continual conflict between the flesh and the spirit (our God-consciousness). If we compare human life to a seed, as Jesus did in His parable, we can say that the flesh (carnal nature) is the outer coating, shell, or husk. It tries to envelop and imprison the embryo or kernel, which we can liken to the spirit. When the seed is planted, the coating dies. It breaks open, and the life inside bursts out! Spiritually, when we die to the flesh, becoming broken before God, then our inner spiritual life, which is from God, flows out.

The anointing can flow from God to us, and then from us to others.

Another way to speak of this inner spiritual life is the anointing. When the anointing flows, we can minister to others. An anointed person releases the life of God to others. Such a person is so full of God's Spirit that he can no longer contain Him. When we pour water into a glass, it will soon become full. If we continue to pour, the glass will overflow and the water will spill over the rim. So it is with the person who is full of the life of God.

Isaiah 10:27 says that "the yoke shall be destroyed because of the anointing." When we become broken before God, we release our faith and allow the Holy Spirit to work freely in our lives. The anointing can flow from God to us, and then from us to others. Yokes of bondage will be destroyed because of the anointing. The anointing will bring healing.

The woman in Luke 7 wept tears, and then she wiped them with her hair. Why did she not use her robe or skirt, which was long and full? According to I Corinthians 11:10, a woman with long hair has "power," or a symbol of authority, on her head, "because of the angels." Under the leadership of God and of her husband, she has authority in the spiritual realm that is evident to the angels, both good and evil.

As an illustration in the natural realm, suppose a small policewoman is in the middle of an intersection directing traffic because the lights are out. A monstrous eighteen-wheeler barrels down the road directly at her, and she motions for it to stop because a Volkswagen is waiting to turn. The truck driver does not insist on his own way but rolls to a stop. It is not because he is afraid of the police-woman but because he recognizes the authority behind the uniform she is wearing. He knows that if he ignores her directions, he will be forced to reckon with a power much higher and mightier than she.

Likewise, the children of God wear uniforms of right-eousness. The demons recognize our identity and the power and authority behind it. According to I Corinthians 11:15, part of that identification is our hair: "But if a woman have long hair, it is a glory to her: for her hair is given her for a covering." When a godly woman drops to her knees she has assurance that her prayers will be effective because she has the authority to go to God.

For the woman in Luke 7, her hair was her glory. We

know it was long and flowing, for she had enough hair to wipe the Lord's feet with it. Thus her glory literally became a rag to wipe the feet of Jesus. She humbled herself completely before Him. She cared for nothing but Jesus!

We must share Jesus! That means telling others about Him, but it means far more. Sharing Jesus is not only talking about Him; it is being like Him. When we are among people, they must experience Him in our presence. Only by seeing less of us, and more of Him, will they ever feel their need for a Savior through us.

When our outer shell is broken, the character of Jesus Christ is released to minister, to bring life to others. But how is the shell broken? There are a number of ways for the natural seed. Soil, temperature, and humidity all work together to force the shell to open up. External pressures work on the seed to release its inner life.

Likewise, outside forces can cause us to die to self and to seek God. That is why it is so important for us to evaluate our circumstances and respond to them rather than react to them.

Prayer opens the shell. Likewise, worship can open the shell, but we must learn to worship in the right way. Psalm 22:3 says that God inhabits the praises of His people, but we should recognize that as Spirit-filled believers we already have Him dwelling within us. We do not worship to bring Him down *to* us; we worship to let Him *out of* us! Our worship, therefore, needs to bring us to a place of surrender and brokenness. When that happens, then the Spirit of God inside of us is released.

How can we know if we are broken? Sometimes we labor under the illusion of being broken when we actually are not. A good test is to examine our behavior in church.

As we sit in our comfortable padded pews, do we drool at the thought of hurrying off to Shoney's after service? Are we preoccupied with meeting our friends, laughing, and having a good time. There is nothing wrong with fellowship; it is a vital part of our lives, and we need it. Many times I have been starved for the fellowship of people of like precious faith. But what about time for prayer at the close of the worship service? When the preacher has made the appeal to pray, do we hurry out? Do we leave others praying at the altar?

If we are broken, we find ourselves among the last to leave the altar. We weep and pray for others. We worship. We gaze into the wonderful face of our God. We only want to be alone with God. That is how we know we have been broken and are ready to be used by God.

Chapter 18

Bearing the Cross

Suffering is something that inevitably happens on a cross. And Jesus told us to take up our cross daily and follow Him. (Seek Luke 9:23-24.) God is a Father who wants only the best for His children. Sometimes—oftentimes—suffering is best. But He never asks us to do anything that He Himself has not done.

As we studied in the last chapter, we must die daily. (See I Corinthians 15:31.) The cross is an instrument of death. Jesus said, "He that taketh not his cross, and followeth after me, is not worthy of me. He that findeth his life shall lose it: and he that loseth his life for my sake shall find it" (Matthew 10:38-39). (See also Matthew 16:24-25.)

When Jesus suffered on the cross, He gave us an example of how we are to suffer. On the cross, He prayed for others, He forgave others, He took care of His mother, and He kept His mind on the will of God. He took His mind off the temporal, the carnal, the fleshly and placed it on eternal things. He focused on the work He needed to accomplish, the reason for His coming to earth in the first place.

Of course, the reason for the Cross was to redeem us from sin. But while on the cross, Jesus not only died for the sins of the world, He also ministered to those nearby and gave us an example to follow when we carry our own crosses. He reached out and ministered from the cross because it was His nature to do so. God is love, and love cannot be denied. Jesus, in spite of all the pain and suffering, was still love incarnate, and He could not do anything less.

Too often we yell out to God, "Get me down! Get me out of this pain!" What we need to say is, "I am doing a good work. I will *not* come down!" (See Nehemiah 6:3.)

As I look back over painful experiences in my life, I consider them to be crosses that God allowed me to carry to further His purpose in my life. Unfortunately, they were crosses I often refused to bear. Instead I cried out, "Lord I can't handle this, it hurts too bad!" And so I put down the cross. I did not understand that suffering helps to develop our lives. I thought if I suffered, then I was doing something wrong.

The pain of being neglected and abandoned is one of the hardest pains to bear. My own children still struggle with this pain. Their dad left when Joseph was seven; Julie was eleven. There were no phone calls, no postcards, nothing. How deeply they hurt! How they must have struggled silently through hurt, bitterness, anger, confusion! All over the world, children are abandoned by their parents. I have experienced that same pain.

But I have a God who knows what is best for me. He planned my life from my beginning. He stooped down to the deep, dark pit in which I struggled—a hopeless drunk, a deserted wife—and made something out of me. He made me a person who can be used in His glorious kingdom. If He can do it for me, He can do it for anybody!

Instrument of Death

The cross is an instrument of death. Bearing our cross encompasses a lot more than a specific instance of suffering in our lives. To take up our cross, we must surrender our lives to the plan of God. We must become "obedient unto death" (Philippians 2:8). We must "die daily" (I Corinthians 15:31). And this is where we balk. We do not like death! We do not want to die—especially not every day! Once is enough, and that is too many!

That is one reason things like suicide, abortion, and euthanasia are so difficult for us to deal with. They mean death, and we avoid death because it is such an uncomfortable subject.

How Do We Die Daily?

The question is, How do we die daily?

One way we learn to die, or submit to the will of God, is through circumstances. Life is our school; it is the university of the soul.

When we go to school, we have assignments. We have work to do in class and work to do at home. We have to complete all our assignments, or we do not pass the course. When I was working for my undergraduate degree in psychology, I had to take statistics. I hated statistics! Combinations and permutations—what good were these things when someone's heart was breaking? I never understood statistics. It is needed for certain types of research, the kind of research I would never be doing once I got out of university. Still, two semesters of statistics were required.

The question is, How do we die daily?

That is like our school with God. We have many required courses. We do not understand why we need them; they do not make a bit of sense to us. But still we have to take them, and pass them, because they are part of the requirements.

To get a bachelor's degree, I was supposed to take biology. The course description told me I would have to cut up mice and cats, and I knew right then I was going to be a college dropout! I went to my adviser. She told me I had to take the course.

"But it says I have to cut up animals."

"How else," she wondered, "will you see what's inside of them?"

"I don't care about what's inside of them. I can look at pictures in a book."

At that point I figured I would never get that degree. But my adviser told me I could substitute botany for biology. She warned, however, "Your education just will not be the same. There will be some holes that will never be filled without biology."

I did not care. I signed up for botany and delighted in every little wildflower I crushed between the pages of a great big book. I passed two semesters of botany, crushed a lot of flowers, learned a lot of Latin names, and eventually got the bachelor's degree.

Sometimes God allows substitutions. If we kick and fuss too much, He quits striving with us. Most of the time, we find ourselves coming back again and again to His assigned courses. If we do not learn the lesson the first time, God brings us back again. Substitutions are second best, and sometimes God allows us to take them when we refuse His very best. But there will be holes, as my adviser warned, that will never be filled.

His Example

As we have discussed, when Jesus hung on the cross He set an example for us by ministering to the needs around Him. He also confessed His own human weakness, pain, and feeling of spiritual abandonment. Nevertheless, He kept His focus on the eternal plan of God.

So must we focus on God and His plan, learning to die to self. We learn to minister to others as we suffer daily on our crosses in our circumstances. If we can forget our pain long enough to reach out and minister to someone else, we will experience strength and joy that only Christ can give. It always happens when we get outside of ourselves and focus on someone else.

It is the devil's job to see that our spiritual eyes remain turned in to ourselves. It is hard, when we hurt, to think of someone else. But that is healing balm. To minister to someone else out of our own suffering, is to bring healing to them—and to us. That is the biggest reason Alcoholics Anonymous (AA) works. Its success does not lie primarily in its twelve steps, or its philosophy, but in reaching out to others through what is called being a "sponsor."

Forgiveness

Perhaps the hardest work to do on a cross is to forgive those who have hurt us. But ministering forgiveness to our enemies brings healing to our own soul and spirit.

When my husband left me, anger and bitterness set in. Months down the road as I began to experience the healing of some forgiveness, it began to dawn on me that my children were the ones to suffer most. There I went again, struggling with hate and bitterness. I had to forgive, then forgive some more. He never knew if I forgave him or not, but God knows. And so do I.

From the cross, Jesus cried out words that bring conviction to our own hearts: "Father, forgive them, for they know not what they do" (Luke 23:34). "The thieves also, which were crucified with him, cast the same in his teeth" (Matthew 27:44). Both the thieves joined in the torture of our King as He hung on the cross. But then, in Luke 23:39-42, we read that there was a change in one thief's attitude. The same thief who had tormented Jesus later defended Him. Finally, he asked that the Lord remember him in the kingdom to come.

Something happened at Calvary to change this man's

HELP ME HEAL

mind. For hours he persecuted the Lord. Then something opened his eyes and led him to repentance. His heart changed as he watched Jesus over His last hours, as he watched a man who was bleeding and dying minister to others in love.

We have to remember that others are watching us. How do we respond to suffering? If we do not have something that our unsaved neighbors do not have, then why should they seek it?

We must forgive those who hurt us.

So the thief finally turned and asked the Lord to remember him. His response to this humble plea was forgiveness, love, and compassion. Jesus ministered to this thief, promising him paradise. What an example for us!

We must forgive as He did. Jesus would not require us to do something impossible. We must forgive those who hurt us. We must forgive those who abuse us. If we do not, we will not be able to take our eyes off our pain and focus them on things eternal. We will come down from our cross.

As we will discuss in chapter 21, we must forgive in order to be forgiven. (See Matthew 6:14-15.) We learn to forgive by the hurts we suffer.

Self-will

Being crucified with Christ involves killing our self-will. (See Galatians 5:24.) One of the most important lessons we can learn about crucifying self-will, is the lesson of silence. There are times when we are not to defend ourselves.

Jesus remained silent on the cross when we would have screamed out in our own defense. He who enjoined-modesty all throughout His Word was stretched naked on a cross while others stared at Him. "And sitting down they watched him there" (Matthew 27:36). I would have wept and probably screamed, but He remained silent. "And they that passed by reviled him, wagging their heads, and saying . . ." (Matthew 27:39-40). The onlookers had much to say in ridicule as He hung suspended between earth and heaven. They challenged Him to come down from the cross: "If thou be the Son of God come down from the cross. Likewise also the chief priests mocking him, with the scribes and elders, said, He saved others; himself he cannot save. If he be the King of Israel, let him now come down from the cross, and we will believe him" (Matthew 27:40-42). They spoke these words, not out of faith that He could do so, but to mock. Again Jesus remained silent. If I had been the Messiah, I would have found it most difficult not to come down from the cross and show them who I really was.

As He hung there naked, bleeding, suffering, and dying, Jesus looked upon Mary, His mother, with deep concern. (See John 19:25-27.) He had to take care of His mother. He commended her to the disciple whom He loved: "Woman, behold thy son." Jesus was taking care of others—always ministering, reaching out, even from the cross.

A Perfect Plan

As Jesus hung on the cross, it seemed that He had lost this battle. The bystanders gave Him the opportunity to come down from the cross in order to save Himself and to prove that He could do it. Jesus could have called down ten thousand angels to rescue Him, but He did not. He knew that He could only fulfill the perfect plan of God by staying on the cross.

We too have the choice of accepting or rejecting our cross. We can be delivered from our cross—for the time being. But eventually, we will have to face the decision again to take up the cross, and it may be even more difficult the next time.

Furthermore, if we choose to be rescued from the cross, what happens to those who are looking at us? Some, like the thief on the cross, may be won to God by our choice to submit to the cross.

Eventually, if we remain true to God, we will have to learn the lessons that the cross has for us. We will let Him develop in us a character that is like Him. Romans 8:29 tells us our life goal is to be conformed to His image. He will mold us, if we let Him. He will take all our experiences, including suffering, and work them together to accomplish His purpose.

I took pills to commit suicide and ended up in a mental hospital. I cannot think of any learning experience more depressing than Mental Hospital 101. But God let me take that road, hoping I would seek Him. Unfortunately, I did not. I could have turned to the only One who truly cared for me, but I was afraid to. I was afraid He too would abandon me.

He wanted me to come back to him, to stop running from His call on my life. But instead of turning to God, I turned to the field of psychology. After getting my master's degree, I was accepted in a prestigious private university in California. I loaded up my children, and we took off for another adventure.

I was raised in a strict Southern Baptist tradition, always involved in everything at church. In my teens, however, I drifted from the church and began a worldly life. I committed much sin, but God was still on the sidelines patiently waiting. He was there all the time.

Later on I ran from church to church, searching. Eventually I became a leader in the humanistic New Age movement, still searching for the God of my childhood.

When I was nine years old, a powerful message in the Baptist church touched my heart. In the dimly lit auditorium, I walked down the aisle in response to the altar call. It was a solemn day for me, a day of deep consecration and dedication to my Lord. "I surrender all!" I cried. "Dear Jesus, take my hand and hold me close! I have so many fears, my Lord!" I was afraid of people, afraid of the dark, afraid of strangers, afraid of drunken uncles, afraid of death, afraid of broken legs, afraid of failing my mother, afraid of failing God. In spite of everything, I decided to follow Jesus, to give Him my life, my soul.

From the depths of my being, I cried out to God and dedicated my life to Him, pitiful though it was. Whatever He wanted, I would do. At the front of the church, upon shaking the pastor's hand, I asked the Lord to reveal to me what He would have me do. I determined to read the Bible through before the next Sunday and opened it to Genesis 1. By Genesis 10, I laid it down in discouragement.

Let me share some of the experiences of my life that in retrospect I see as opportunities to take up my cross and follow Jesus. Unfortunately, I mishandled them, but through these experiences I eventually learned to seek God. My hope is that others can learn from them as well.

Failure

At age seven, I remember thinking, Where is Daddy? He was in a long black car, and Mama was screaming and screaming and screaming. Flowers were everywhere; I smelled the sickening sweet scent of carnations. I heard weeping and mournful singing and saw a large, silver box. Then he disappeared into a hideous black hole, never to be seen again.

Why did he leave? I wondered What did I do wrong? Did I do something to make him angry? And on top of that, I made Mama angry, too. I bothered her with my own petty problems in her time of need.

I believed I had failed my daddy, or he would not have

left me. I went into denial, and mistakenly I determined not to fail anyone else ever again.

Abandonment

At age eleven, the one man in my life who really cared about me was long, tall Granddaddy, the county sheriff. I was so proud of him in his handsome uniform. He loved me so much that he would let me sit on his lap, watch him sharpen his saws, and share his whiskey. Oh, how I loved Granddaddy! I was so starved for love and attention that I learned to love the whiskey, too. He did not know that I would someday become an alcoholic.

And now he was dying. No! I couldn't make it without Granddaddy!

In the deep of the winter I stumbled around to the corner grocery store, trying anything to clear my thoughts. Christmas carols were playing everywhere, eyes twinkling, people hugging and laughing and wishing one another a merry Christmas. What was wrong with them? my heart cried. Didn't they know? Didn't they care? Granddaddy was dying. Granddaddy was leaving me. How could the world go on as though nothing was happening?

On New Year's Day he died. Again I had failed. This time I mistakenly responded with bitterness. I had vowed never to fail anyone again, yet I thought I had failed the most important person in my life. Granddaddy had left me, too.

Humiliation

My thirteenth birthday was the big one! Finally! I would be a bona-fide teenager! Mama said I could have a party, and I was beside myself with anticipation. At the top of my list was the most important name of all: Kate, the most popular girl in my school. Everyone on my list had promised to be there, including the student body president and the fullback of the football team. I did not care about politics, and I certainly did not care about football, but I did care about the cute guys!

Well, five o'clock came, then five thirty, and then six. No one showed up.

Where did I get the nerve to invite these big shots, anyway? I berated myself. Who did I think I was? My thirteen-year-old heart was crushed, and I knew I would never be the same again. There was no worse way to begin my teenage years than to give a party and have nobody come. I sobbed myself to sleep that night, and a big chunk of my heart froze over. This time I handled my cross by closing off my spirit.

The deep pain and devastation these events caused in my heart could be traced back to my first few years of rejection, neglect, and abuse. Then in later years, seeking love and approval, I drifted into alcoholism, prescription drug abuse, and the New Age. I became an important figure in my part of the New Age movement—a channeler. The world lay at my feet as I led an organization whose purpose was to build a teaching center in northern California.

God would not let me remain in this mess, however. He let my world begin to fall apart, until my entire life had crashed down around me. I no longer had cigarettes . . . alcohol . . . marijuana . . . sex . . . prescription drugs . . . or even suicide—to help me cope. I finally came face to face with myself, and I hated what I saw. I spent a solid week repenting to the God of my childhood—somehow I knew He was the One who could save me. Somehow, my soul had a knowledge that this God knew how to lead me into life if I could just somehow touch Him and tap into His power.

After a week of sorrowfully crying out to God (which I later came to know was repentance), I went up a mountain to a place called Willow Creek. There, sitting on a tree stump, I felt clean and free. Repentance had removed from me all the ugliness of my life. On that beautiful sunny May day, I felt the hand of God caress my cheek in the form of a gentle breeze. I heard the whistling of the leaves over my head, and as I looked up I saw them waving to me in the breeze. It was almost as though the leaves were dancing with an unspeakable joy. As I watched the sun filtering through the branches, my heart lifted to my God. I had never heard of raising hands in praise and worship, but that is what I did. I lifted my hands along with my heart and whispered, "Thank You, God, for the love You're giving me right this minute. Thank You for cleansing me and forgiving me."

When I did that, I began to speak in another language as He filled me with His glorious Holy Spirit, right there on the tree trunk by the creek in the California wilderness. What joy! Jesus rescued me.

My life was totally transformed in that one afternoon on the banks of Willow Creek.

For a week after that, I went around saying, "I'm drunk with it; I'm drunk with it." I did not know anything about the Holy Spirit, but I knew that I felt drunk with whatever it was.

No one understood. They were worried that I had gone off the deep end for sure this time. As for me, my life was totally transformed in that one afternoon on the banks of Willow Creek.

We need to be willing to give everything to Jesus. We should not take anything as our own; all that we have is on loan from Him. Let us give it all to Him, so we do not have to learn the hard way through experiences that take it from us.

Exposure to the Light

When a person finally exposes the deepest areas of his life that have caused fear, bitterness, or rejection of memory, then the exposure to light by open confession brings healing. Satan operates in the past, but Christ operates in the present and future. The key to healing is to be open and transparent with God. Doing so destroys the power of the enemy to accuse our conscience before God. (See Revelation 12:10.)

When a person is broken before the Lord and does not go into denial, or try to run away and shut God out, or to accuse God and murmur and complain, something beautiful happens. The roots of bitterness and unforgiveness will be removed from his innermost being, and the waters of his soul will be cleansed of impurities. Victory is certain.

When we begin to break before God, and when we ask God to break us, He will cleanse our memories. This healing process requires open confession. We must get all of the ugliness out of the dark places of our soul. We, like Jesus, must become transparent and vulnerable. Jesus openly confessed feelings of abandonment as He cried from the cross, "My God, my God, why has thou forsaken me?" He did not care that others, including His enemies, knew that He felt forsaken.

Sunscreen

When we have taken up the cross, exposed ourselves to the light, confessed our sins and hurts to God, and yet not found complete relief, we should ask God what our sunscreen is. Something is standing in the way, and that something could very well be unforgiveness. We must purpose to get all garbage and all sun blocks out of the way. We must be completely honest with both God and ourselves.

The Christian walk is progressive. God gives us enough light to take a step at a time. When we are faithful to the light He has given us, then it is time to move on to bigger, more fertile grounds. It seems that God always has something more—something better—for us, even when we might be content with what we already have.

Chapter 19

⌒

Steps to Healing

We sat in the front seat of her van in the church parking lot, the rain drizzling softly against the windows. It was a chilly New Orleans day, chilly and wet, with the sun coming out from time to time. It would get warm enough to turn on the air conditioner and then suddenly drop again to a near-freezing cold.

"Sister Allison," she said, "we need teaching about what it means to be healed."

She got my attention fast. What did she mean, people needed teaching? You're healed or you're not, I thought. At the same time, I felt the Holy Ghost in that car. God was trying to get my attention. This was a leader speaking, and I respected her opinions highly. "Go on," I responded. "What kind of teaching?"

She proceeded to explain. "We know we're supposed to pray and read the Bible. And sometimes we talk about what's hurting. We know to wait on God, and we know all those things we should be doing. Usually we fall short, and then we feel guilty, and . . . Sister Allison, I don't know how it feels. How does healing *feel*?"

I really hated to show my ignorance. "Well . . ."

"I mean, how do we know if we're on track? How do we know we're going in the right direction? Aren't there some kind of guidelines we can follow? What happens if we think we're healed, and then we come to find out that we're not. Not really. Something else pops up. There is so much discouragement! That's why some people are just giving up."

I realized that what she was saying was true. I felt dazed. "I don't know. I never thought of such a thing. Keep talking."

She did, and I listened. To me, it was a new idea: people need to know what healing *feels* like. They need signposts to indicate that they are on the right road. I left her that day asking her to pray for me that God would teach me and anoint me so I could get something down on paper. She profusely promised her prayers.

I have come to understand that not all healing comes in one moment. Not all those with cancer, for example, receive healing the instant they are prayed for. Sometimes we see miracles of instantaneous healing, such as the bent back straightened, the tumor falling off, and the wheelchair left behind. That is what we like to see, and that is what most of us are looking for in our own healing. When it does not happen that way, we often get discouraged and think we have not been healed.

More often than not, healing is accomplished gradually. The Bible assures us that if we receive prayer and anointing with oil, we shall be healed. Sometimes we do not recognize the answer to this prayer. Sometimes, for example, as influenza is healed gradually over a period of a week, we do not give God the credit and the glory. If we want to see greater revival, miracles, signs, and wonders, we must be willing to give God the glory for what He has already done. An unthankful heart receives little from the Lord.

Many times we receive emotional healing but do not recognize it. Because the healing did not come instantly, we continue our daily life as though nothing happened, as though we are still as wounded and helpless as before.

The truth is, we often receive healing by degrees.

After we have received a degree of healing, we need to thank God, giving Him praise, honor, and glory. We also need to believe Him. We must trust that He has done a work, that He will continue to do a work, and that we need to enjoy what He has just given us.

The Bible says that nothing is too hard for the Lord. (See Jeremiah 32:17.) The shattered life that results from abuse is not too hard for the Lord to heal in one instant—and often He does. That is why we find people in our churches with a background of abuse and yet they do not live dysfunctionally. God healed them instantaneously.

Lorrie Lenaghen, director of Wings of Love ministry, agrees that healing is usually a process: "I wouldn't say the entire healing process has been painless or easy. Rather, like any process, there are good and bad days along the journey. Before I allowed my heart to be opened and my past spilled on the altar, I felt as if I would carry my hurt to the grave. I've seen many women, burdened by guilt, destroy their lives with suicide, alcohol, promiscuity, depression, and other destructive behavior. I traveled that road for many years, and believe me, God's grace is sufficient to deliver."

It is important to realize that we may receive our healing as part of a process, by degrees; otherwise we could be swallowed up by guilt, condemnation, and hopelessness because we have not been instantly healed. As Dorian Joseph said, "Now all of this did not happen overnight. Nevertheless, I can tell you that God is a perfect gentleman; He did not heal any area of my life that I was not willing to allow Him to enter into."

At least part of the reason why we receive healing over a period of time instead of instantly is because of ourselves. We are not ready. We are not willing to allow Him into certain places. But healing will come. We must not be discouraged!

To Those Who Have Been Healed Instantly

If God has healed you instantly, please do not lose patience with those of us who are healed in stages or degrees. It has done so much harm for someone to say, "Well you've got the Holy Ghost now; you need to just forget all the other. I went through abuse, too, but I've just put it all behind me." Please, do not say this to a hurting brother or sister! Doing so adds abuse on top of abuse. If you are unable to work with a certain hurting person and bathe them with compassionate prayer, then just step aside. Do not offer your "advice."

One example is a young woman I worked with several years ago. She had had seven abortions. I taught her a Bible study, she fell in love with the truth, was baptized, and received the Holy Ghost. At first she did well, but soon I noticed some disturbing symptoms. For example, every now and then, I would discern a flash of rebellion and anger. I confronted her with this and, with some probing, she admitted it. That is when she told me about the abortions.

Knowing what I know about *one* abortion, I knew this lady had to have some biblical counseling. Her pastor, however, believed that receiving the Holy Ghost was all one needed. He refused to let her have counseling. "The Holy Ghost is enough," he said. The Holy Ghost *is* enough. The Holy Ghost is *more* than enough. The fault does not lie with the Holy Ghost; the fault lies with us. Sometimes we have misconceptions and unhealthy feelings that godly counseling can help correct so that we are open to the work of the Holy Ghost.

I watched as she began to grow hard and cold with anger and rebellion. She soon experienced what some people call a nervous breakdown. She tried valiantly, but there was just so much unresolved pain inside of her. She finally just quit trying. Today she is as far from God as a person can be, and the situation breaks my heart.

Receiving the Holy Ghost is the most beautiful thing in the world. The Spirit is absolutely necessary for salvation, for growth, for serving God. We cannot do without the Holy Ghost. But receiving the Holy Ghost is just the beginning; it is not the ending.

Some of the previous chapters have dealt with our attitudes toward suffering and pain. As we have discussed, it is vital that we have a change in the way we see things, that we learn to see this life from God's perspective.

Now we will discuss some specific steps for healing. This list of steps will be difficult to accomplish without the information contained in the rest of the book. It is my prayer that no one will turn to this chapter and attempt to find healing from a list. The details of how to fulfill this list are found throughout the book. With this admonition in mind, let us look at some specific steps for healing:

1. *Take your pain out of darkness and into light*. Talk about it to a trusted person.

2. *Pray*. Take your pain to God. Talk to Him about it. Get out all your feelings. If you are angry at God, tell Him so. You do not want to blaspheme Him, but you can talk to Him honestly about your feelings for He already knows about them anyway. These ugly feelings are like the ugly pus in a wound; they have to come out.

3. *Take your pain to the person who hurt you by writing a letter*. It is too early to face the person with the truth. Tell them of your feelings in a letter, and tell them that you plan to forgive them totally.

4. *Take your pain and the letter to the altar*. Ask God to help you forgive this person. (See chapter 21.) You must forgive, for if you do not forgive then you cannot be forgiven and you cannot enter heaven. No one is worth losing heaven over! Forgiveness does not mean justifying or ignoring the wrong that someone has done. If they had not wronged us, we would not be expected to

forgive. Forgiveness means choosing to let go of your bitterness, hatred, and ill will. It means wanting to see that person make things right with God and with you, and being willing to respond mercifully if the person does so. Think this step over carefully and ask God to help you. Forgiveness is the most important step of all.

5. *Take your pain to worship.* Each time you feel the pain, lift your hands and worship God. Praise Him, love Him, and thank Him. Concentrate on His sovereignty, goodness, faithfulness, and power. Concentrate on His being the Good Shepherd and the Great Physician. See Him as He suffered on the cross, bleeding and dying for you.

6. *If the person who hurt you is still alive, and you are comfortable with doing so, arrange to talk to him.* Tell him how much he hurt you but that you forgive him. Many times the offender will not admit his sin. Many offenders remain forever in denial. Sometimes he will confess, and healing can then take place for both of you. Whether he confesses or not, however, keep the meeting brief. Do not linger or debate the issue. Do not allow him to lay guilt on you. He is the one who is guilty, not you.

Walk in Your Healing

7. *Walk in your new healing.* Enjoy it. Thank and praise the Lord every day for the work He has done in you. This is the step that my friend in New Orleans said she did not recognize. How do you know when you have completed a phase of your healing? What does it mean to walk in your healing?

Listen. Each day focus on the beauty that surrounds you. Listen intently to the birds and the lovely song on the radio. Walk around the neighborhood, taking in all the details of the houses and their yards. What you are doing is unfreezing your emotions after so many years of being shut down. You have to train yourself to really feel again.

Feel! Experience your senses! Take a bubble bath and really and truly enjoy it. Read a book simply for the pleasure of reading it, not for escape or for education. Be aware of any discomfort you might feel in your emotions, but try to focus on the sheer joy of living. If you feel any of the old pain, pray and worship until you overcome it. If you feel any of the old anger toward your offender, take it back to the altar again. Each time you forgive, even the same person for the same offense, healing comes. You take another step closer to the wholeness that the Lord has for you.

8. *Be alert to any feelings that spring up*, such as unexpected anger, a new compulsive behavior like excessive shopping or overeating, or a new phobia. These kinds of things could indicate that more healing is on the way. God may be getting ready to reveal another area that needs to be healed.

If so, do not be discouraged. Do not despair because you thought you were healed but now find that really you are not. On the contrary, recognize that you have received healing and are now ready to receive more healing. Each new phase is another step to wholeness. Enjoy each healing as it comes. Let your heart be filled with praise and thanksgiving. The key lies in having joy in the Lord.

"A Merry Heart Doeth Good Like a Medicine"

9. *Find out what makes you laugh.* (See Proverbs 17:22.) No matter how bad you might feel, somewhere there is something that makes you laugh. When I needed healing, I searched for something to make me laugh, and I just could not seem to find anything. I enjoyed "I Love Lucy" reruns and "Mr. Magoo," but I did not have access to video equipment and certainly not television (which causes far more harm than any good it might bring). I sought the Lord about this, for He created me and certainly knows what would make me laugh.

Soon, I found myself laughing and giggling for no apparent reason. At first I did not recognize this new attitude as an answer to my prayer. Often, however, something would strike me as funny, and because my laughter was not directed at someone else's behavior, no one took offense. Because it was from the Lord, others were able to laugh with me.

I found myself laughing and giggling for no apparent reason.

Recently I got a giggle spell while my husband was saying the blessing at dinner. Inwardly I was horrified; it felt so disrespectful, but I could not stop giggling. He continued to say the blessing, and then I mumbled, "I'm so sorry, honey, I don't mean to be disrespectful!" That wonderful, understanding man got up from his place, came to me, and put his arms around me. As I continued to giggle, he also giggled and thanked the Lord for his bride's wonderful laugh. "I love to hear her laughter, Lord! Thank You!" He understands how difficult laughter has been for me, and he understands the healing that rests in laughter.

I am coming to see times like this as "medicine" from the Lord. Ecclesiastes 3:4 tells us there is a time to weep and a time to laugh. We weep in prayer, and we weep when someone else is weeping (Romans 12:15). It is not time to weep every day, hour by hour, although some seem to think so. Proverbs 15:15 tells us, "All the days of the afflicted are evil: but he that is of a merry heart hath a continual feast." "And where the Spirit of the Lord is, there is liberty" (II Corinthians 3:17).

There was a time when I would sit on my judgmental high horse and look down on those who laughed at what I considered to be inappropriate times. I am coming to understand that God has a tremendous sense of humor.

He sometimes administers the medicine of laughter in the least likely places and at the least likely times. When we ask God to help us learn to laugh, let us be prepared. He will answer that prayer!

A friend, upon learning of my giggle spells, brought me a Bible verse. "This is yours," she said. I followed her finger to Genesis 21:6: "And Sarah said, God hath made me to laugh, so that all that hear will laugh with me." Thank you, Sarah!

We tend to take ourselves too seriously. Whether or not someone agrees with my giggle spells, this one thing we all need to understand: God made us, and God has a sense of humor. Laughter is one of the best healing balms we will find anywhere.

10.   *Finally, if the Lord reveals another area where you need healing, be prepared to repeat the preceding steps.*

Chapter 20

⁓

Pulling Down Strongholds

"For the weapons of our warfare are not carnal, but mighty through God to the pulling down of strong holds" (II Corinthians 10:4).

We now come to the very heart of our study on healing: pulling down strongholds. This is spiritual warfare right where the war is being fought—in our minds! We must get victory over our carnal, distorted thinking. "For to be carnally minded is death; but to be spiritually minded is life and peace" (Romans 8:6).

Psalm 73 illustrates what happens when we do not discover and correct our faulty thinking. Asaph's feet were almost gone; his steps had almost slipped. For sixteen verses, Asaph lamented his poor condition as contrasted with the apparent prosperity of the wicked. He was in a deep depression. In verse 16, he wailed, "When I thought to know this, it was too painful for me."

In passages such as these, the Bible reveals its characters' imperfections as well as their good points. The Bible always tells it just like it is. God knew that one day His children would need to read about others who had suffered as they are presently suffering—and overcome. In the next verse, Asaph gave the secret to victory: "Until

I went into the sanctuary of God: then understood I their end" (Psalm 73:17). The remainder of the psalm goes on to extol God and His great ways, climaxing with Asaph's pure trust in the final verse.

Asaph was not sitting in a counselor's office somewhere, undergoing a therapeutic dialogue. No great therapeutic technique was exercised between verses 16 and 17. The action that changed Asaph's thinking was going to the sanctuary of God. Even there, we do not read that he counseled with a priest or another person. The key for him was a dialogue inside his own head. He prayed. And, as David, Asaph encouraged himself in the Lord. (See I Samuel 30:6.) We must learn to do the same. We must learn to control what we talk about with ourselves inside our heads!

C. S. Lovett told about a time he, Dewey Lockman, and Franklin Logsdon went to see Charles E. Fuller, preacher on the "Old-Fashioned Revival Hour" and founder of Fuller Seminary. In the conversation, the name of a prominent Christian leader was mentioned, one who was then attacking Fuller Seminary. "I shall never forget Brother Fuller's response to the comment this man made about his school," Lovett reported.

"'Yeeesss,' he drawled, 'God bless him.'

"Dr. Logsdon was the quickest to respond, 'You don't seem too upset, Brother Fuller!'

"Then came an astonishing reply: 'Why should I let someone else decide how I am going to act!'" (Lovett, 1968, 71-72).

"As He Thinketh . . ."

We can eliminate a large chunk of our misery by applying a simple principle. While the method itself is simple, it is not always easy to implement. It requires that we change habits of a lifetime, and we cannot expect to do this overnight. Like losing weight, it takes effort. It requires diligence, but it is worth it a hundred times over!

The wise man Solomon declared of a miser, "As he thinketh in his heart, so is he" (Proverbs 23:7). In other words, a person's character and actions are determined by what he thinks. If we want to change our direction, and if we want to assume control over our lives, then we must change our way of thinking. When we do, life can become a joy no matter what our circumstances.

If we want to change our direction, and if we want to assume control over our lives, then we must change our way of thinking.

Paul wrote, "For the weapons of our warfare are not carnal, but mighty through God to the pulling down of strong holds; casting down imaginations, and every high thing that exalteth itself against the knowledge of God, and bringing into captivity every thought to the obedience of Christ" (II Corinthians 10:4-5). From these two verses it is clear that to pull down strongholds we must do something about our thoughts.

The battlefield is in our minds. That is where Satan carries on his warfare against us, and if he can get a stronghold in our minds, he is well on his way to victory. He knows when he has such a stronghold, but most of the time we are not aware of it.

A "stronghold," as we will use the term here, is a cluster of ungodly thoughts that have been used so many times that they have formed into an ugly, tangled knot. The bigger the knot, the bigger the stronghold. Its size depends on how long its maker has been building on it. These strongholds have to be torn down. We tear them down by stopping the ungodly thinking process and working on its opposite: godly, biblical thinking.

Every thought we think leaves its impression on the

cortex of the brain. If we think the same thought constantly, the impression becomes a rut, making it increasingly difficult to reroute our thinking. That is why we must "pull down" and "cast down" strongholds, not just set them aside gently. Doing so is hard work, but it is worth every effort.

Most of our burdens would become lighter if we would only change the way we look at those burdens, if we would lift our eyes to Jesus and see Him at work in the situation. One of the most life-changing principles I ever learned, and am still learning, is that I am in control of what I allow to blossom in my mind.

Have you ever had a pet suggestion vetoed or a favorite project scrapped? Has the Sunday school superintendent refused to implement those changes you know will make for a better department?

How do we handle setbacks like these? Many people react with feelings of helplessness, guilt, resentment, or depression. Let us take a hypothetical example.

A Cold, Rainy Night

It is your twenty-fifth anniversary, one of the most important days in your life. You have planned this occasion for a long time. When it finally arrives, your husband, John, goes out of town on business and leaves you alone. He cannot take you along with him because he is traveling with his boss and several other men. How do you react? Do you get angry? Resentful?

You're all alone, trying to cheer yourself up, but it is cold outside. On top of that, it is raining. The weather just makes everything seem worse. You sit there and think for a while about how you *always* get depressed in this kind of weather.

Note the word *always*. It is usually a tip-off to what cognitive therapists call "automatic thinking." What you need to realize is that it is not the cold rainy night that is causing the depression; it is not even that you are *alone* on the cold rainy night. It is how you *perceive* being alone on a cold, rainy night. What, exactly, are you telling yourself about this situation? Are you saying something like this: "Why did John have to go and leave me tonight? He *should have* [another tip-off] realized that I need to have him home on our anniversary!"

Thus, it is not our circumstances that control our behavior; it is what we *believe* about those circumstances. "If John loved me," you might say to yourself on that lonely night, "he would not have gone off and left me by myself." That implies that you are unloved by John. Look where this self-conversation is heading. If something is not done to put the brakes on this kind of thinking, soon the self-pity will develop into bitterness. "Just wait till he wants me to do something for him; I'll show him." Here we have the "root of bitterness" mentioned in Hebrews 12:15.

If our thoughts create our emotions and then our emotions create our behavior, what can we do to create change in our lives? We can change our emotions by changing our thoughts.

But wait . . .

Not All Situations Are Meant to Be Changed

Alcoholics use a prayer called the "Serenity Prayer" that should be a part of everyone's daily attitude: "God grant me the serenity to accept the things I cannot change, the courage to change the things I can, and the wisdom to know the difference." Some things simply are not meant to be changed. Some things are offered to us by God's loving hand to train us and teach us. Some things are a part of His perfect plan for our lives. We need only accept these things, say, "Thank You, Jesus," and march on. We have covered these kinds of circumstances elsewhere in this book.

Some things are simply a part of life and we must accept those, too. If John, for example, absolutely must go out of town, it is destructive for his wife to insist that he stay with her to celebrate their anniversary. If he tried to work out an alternative and was not able to, then she must accept the circumstances.

Paul encountered one of these situations with "a thorn in the flesh." He sought God three times about removing it. Finally God said, in essence, "No, this is a situation I want you to learn to live with; I have a purpose for it." So Paul changed his thinking about the thorn. He accepted it, he thanked God for giving him grace sufficient to bear it, and he thanked God for areas of weakness that allowed him to become strong in the Lord. (See II Corinthians 12:7-10.)

Those situations we cannot change become golden opportunities for us to change ourselves.

Those situations we cannot change become golden opportunities for us to change ourselves—by interpreting them in a different way, a positive and fulfilling way. But we must be prepared to fail a few times. It requires much hard work to bring our thoughts into captivity, as II Corinthians 10:5 instructs. When the negative thinking comes, we must stop it and begin to quote Scripture. Or we can replace the negative thought with an opposite one such as "I can!" instead of "I could never do that."

Paul gave more life-changing advice in Philippians 4:8, when he said to practice thinking on the good things. Going back to that lonely anniversary, it is easy to see that the wife was getting into a pattern of *generalized thinking*. She found herself thinking, John doesn't love me, period, because he wasn't here this one night. She generalized the one event to include the entire relationship. Instead she could say, "I know John loves me." Or, "Just last week he brought me flowers." And, "He sent me that darling little card with the teddy bear on the front." Immediately she will feel better! "He's always calling from the office just to tell me he loves me." From this example, we see how important one's *focus* is.

With this new way of thinking, gradually the night will grow sweeter. The wife begins to feel loved again. Her strength returns. As she thinks of little things she can do when John comes back, enthusiasm returns to her life. Excitement mounts as she begins planning for his home-coming.

She has just achieved victory!

Our thoughts, then, *do* make a difference! The pattern of our thinking can alter the course of our entire life. Our goal should be to discover our purpose by obeying our Maker at each stage, fixing our gaze and thoughts on Him and then following steadfastly where He leads.

Godly Thinking versus Positive Thinking

"The fallacy of the positive thinking movement is not positive thinking. The fallacy is in getting positive too soon. If we do not get our motivation from God, put our 'success' under God, we might be in for trouble. It is not enough to simply start a day saying, 'I'm going to be positive, I am going to get victory over this, I am determined to think only positive thoughts.' I—I—*I*! God may choose not to add his blessings to our human methodology when the same human methodology phased him out of the planning" (Cook, 1974, 65).

William Cook spoke about an unsaved person telling himself positive things about his spiritual condition, and Cook asked the question: Does positive thinking change his relationship to God? Is he now God's child? "If a carpenter makes a pulpit stand for a church, can it be said that the pulpit is his child? The piece of furniture is his product, not his child. There's a great deal of difference between being one of God's products and one of God's children. As it would be necessary to be born into the family of a carpenter to be the child of a carpenter, so it is necessary to be born into the family of God to be considered God's child. . . . Positive thinking, based on truth, carries fantastic blessing. Getting positive too soon, on the other hand, can do irreparable damage."

Cook continued: "In swimming, I either can or I can't. A thousand times I may tell myself, 'I know I can swim.' If I psyche myself, if I act as if I can when I can't, and jump into the deep water anyway, I may drown.

"In war, I can rush the enemy who outnumbers me 10 to 1, and all the while be acting as if I can whip them all, but the odds are real good that I'll soon be dead.

"In sickness, I can psyche myself and act as if I don't hurt and I may escape 30 percent of the time, but the other 70 percent will scar or kill."

While positive thinking has value, then, it is still limited by our human ability. When we let God control our thinking, however, then it will be not merely positive but godly, and we will have assurance of victory.

The outside world may have control over our body, but no one can control our mind unless we let them. We have complete control over what we choose to think about. We alone control how we react to our circumstances. When we really get this revelation, we will notice a tremendous change in our lives.

The Sources of Distorted Thinking

Webster's Dictionary says that to "distort" means "to twist out of shape, to misrepresent," and "distorted" means "deformed, warped." If we stop to analyze some of the thoughts that pass through our heads, we might be shocked to discover just how warped they really are and how greatly they misrepresent God's Word!

Proverbs 23:7 tells us that, not only is our thought life important, but we *are* what we think. As we will discover, our thinking ultimately determines both our actions and our feelings. It is absolutely imperative that our basic belief system and thinking process be consistent with Scripture.

> *It is absolutely imperative that our basic belief system and thinking process be consistent with Scripture.*

The Scriptures were given as a model and a pattern for our lives. Whether we believe the Scriptures or not, we all proceeded from the same Creator who produced the Scriptures, and it is His plan and design that we all live by these guidelines. The guidelines in this "manual" were written from the heart of God to the heart of humanity. If these guidelines are broken or twisted, suffering results. Guilt, acknowledged or not, is produced. Any thought, then, that does not line up with this manual is distorted, and it must be corrected, changed to line up with the Word of God.

Much of our thinking comes from the corridors of yesteryear—things spoken to us by people long forgotten or loved ones long ago excused. A four-year-old slapped by a drunken uncle and called a little slut may grow up thinking of herself in this light. If she believes on some deep unconscious level that she is a "little slut," then her outward activities may line up with this definition of herself.

Satan can drop thoughts into our minds so convincingly that we can believe they are actually ours. Any time we have a thought that is not according to Scripture, however, we must learn to discard it immediately. We simply must refuse to think about it. I do not go around "rebuking the devil" all the time, but I frequently catch myself saying, "I refuse that thought!" There is an old saying that is very true: You can't stop a bird from flying over your head, but you can prevent him from roosting in your hair. We cannot stop all thoughts from entering our minds, but we can—indeed we must—refuse to entertain them!

Other negative thoughts are "programmed" into us in the form of mental and emotional "tapes" that we have played since childhood. These tapes play automatically in response to both external and internal stimuli. They are quite comfortable because they are so familiar. (I might really like my pretty new pair of shoes, but if I have to walk a lot today, I would rather have my old, comfortable shoes with me.) We have heard these tapes year after year since they were recorded in early life. Although we cannot help what happened to us as children, we can change its effect on our present lives!

Sister Bridgette gives us some insight into what these old tapes can do. She recalls:

"Daily I would unconsciously replay each of my past poor choices and rehearse their equally poor conse- quences. Premature sex, daily drug use, alcohol abuse, poor judgments, no self-esteem, lack of direction, depres- sion, suicide attempts, self-hatred—all of these players were empowered by that grand knight named guilt. I was a prisoner of the war being waged within—with no appar- ent escape. I eventually relegated myself to a mere exis- tence shrouded by unfulfilled dreams and an intense need to punish myself for past mistakes."

Her story illustrates the danger in listening to our evil thoughts. No matter the source—old, forgotten tapes or fresh thoughts from the devil—we must keep a vigilant watch over our thoughts. We must not allow them to wan- der, for a wandering mind is an open invitation to the devil. We must learn to control and discipline our thoughts.

What we feed, grows. Fats and sugars build pounds on

the human body. Bad attitudes and wrong beliefs build strongholds in the human mind. If we choose to entertain that kind of thinking, we will become unhappy and depressed. Our lives will be below what they could and should be. Enough of this kind of thinking might eventually cost us our salvation.

The Need to Uncover Our Core Beliefs

Often we must do more than just change a thought, because as we dig deeper into our modes of thinking we discover that the thoughts are based on a deep-seated, core belief. We need to uncover the core belief in order to expose the underlying need. As an example, I struggled with perfectionism until I tracked down the core belief behind it, namely, "I am not loved and accepted unless I am perfect." That was the belief I had to annihilate. (And I am still working on it!)

Let us take a familiar example: the pastor passes by and does not speak to me. This action itself is not disturbing; it is my core belief that causes distorted thoughts about it and leads to depression. Because my core belief says I am not loved and accepted unless I am perfect, I think that all the other saints are more spiritual than I. Therefore, I reason, my pastor must surely feel that they are more important than I, and I interpret his action in passing by me as a deliberate rejection. If I am not as spiritual as the others, then I am not as good as they are. In order to compensate or measure up, I need to take on even more activities, do even more for God. This kind of activity—perceived as the avenue to the perfection that is required if I am to be accepted and loved—will only end in frustration and more "failure." I am setting myself up for a great depression!

My core belief (I am not loved and accepted unless I am perfect) leads to the thought (I am not as spiritual as the other members), which leads to the behavior (more activity), which leads to disappointing "failure." To break this cycle, the core belief, which goes back to my childhood when nothing I did seemed to please my mother, is what I have to attack.

Since this kind of thinking is so deeply ingrained in us as to make us unaware of its source, we must begin a regimen of diligently monitoring our thinking process. We have to know how God feels about every subject. Again, we have to go by the guidelines of our Maker's manual. We must spend a significant amount of time studying the Word of God. A five-minute devotional reading in the morning, while it does have its place, is not going to get the job done. We have to get so deeply into the Scriptures that they become a part of us. How will we be able to recognize an ungodly thought if we do not have a good understanding of what godly thoughts are?

One recommendation is to follow a plan of reading the entire Bible in one year. A reading chart or a one-year Bible make it simple by setting forth the reading for each day. It is helpful to have a definite place to start each day, rather than just picking up the Bible and thumbing through it. Typically, each day's reading is divided into Old and New Testament chapters, plus a psalm and a proverb. When the Bible becomes our basic diet each day, we will begin to see great things happening in our walk with God. And a one-year reading plan is just the beginning.

What about Feelings?

If we are ever to see consistent answers to our prayers, we must have faith. If we are to be joyful and successful as Christians, the Bible tells us we must walk by faith and not by sight. The biggest hindrance in doing so is allowing our feelings to get in the way. Too often we walk by feelings (sight) and not by faith. We depend on the things we feel and see rather than the Word of God.

Feelings and emotions are neither good nor bad in

themselves; they are a normal part of living and we could not really call ourselves human without them. It is what we do with our feelings that makes the difference—whether or not we allow them to dominate our attitudes and dictate our actions.

Let us consider, for example, a father of three children with a wife who is a full-time homemaker. "I don't feel like working today," he might say. There is nothing wrong with that feeling in itself. There are many days when we do not feel like working. But what does the father do about the feeling? If he chooses to act on it, he becomes irresponsible.

Timothy Foster (1986) speaks of an emotion as being sent from the production line to the packaging and labeling department, where it is a given a name ("I feel hurt . . . ") and an address (". . . at Jane"). He goes on to say that at the factory a new emotion is produced every ten minutes. What would happen if the shipping and delivery department went on strike, but the emotions plant continued to produce emotions? Soon the storeroom would be full, and we would have to start piling boxes inside the factory. The boxes would start to clog the assembly line, and eventually the whole system would shut down.

One of the greatest challenges for most of us is learning to handle our feelings and emotions correctly. Oh, the havoc, the tragedy, the misery, and the wretchedness in the world, simply because people do not know how to handle their own feelings!

Humans are so constituted that feelings have a prominent position in our lives. Our feelings seek to control us, and unless we realize it, they will undoubtedly do so. This is what we mean when we talk about moodiness. A mood may seem to descend upon us. We might not want it, but there it is. Now the danger is in allowing it to control and grip us. We wake up in a bad mood in the morning, and the tendency is to go on like that throughout the day until something happens to put us right. The danger is in submitting ourselves to our feelings and allowing them to dictate to us, to govern and master us, to control our whole lives.

If Sister Bridgette had insisted on going by her feelings and resisted the tug of God, I never would have come to know and love her as I do. But God has done great things in her life! Here is the rest of the story:

"The low road was all I had ever traveled until one day the Lord, knowing exactly where I was, turned up the volume . . . or maybe He just positioned me in a place where I could hear Him as He wooed me to His bosom.

"I later understood that it all began in my mother's womb, where the Lord formed me and called me. His calm hand and keen eye guided me in spite of my quest for self-destruction. God eventually brought me to a small Apostolic church to receive what He had been wanting to give me my whole lifetime. Though sin had seemingly eaten away at my soul like a bad cancer, I still felt the tug of the Holy Spirit. I responded to an altar call, and the next thing I knew, I was speaking in a heavenly language. How marvelous it was!

"For the first time in my life I felt free. I could breathe easier—no pain, no stress, but best of all, no guilt. The Prince of Peace instantly broke the chains of guilt and set me free to be the real me."

We must stand on the Word of God. And to do that, we must spend much time in it. If the only good habit people develop from reading *Help Me Heal* is to begin studying the Word of God, then the book has been worth the effort, for the rest will follow! Let us stay in the Book. Let us conform our thoughts to fit the Book. God will do the rest.

Chapter 21

~

Forgiving Others

"For if ye forgive men their trespasses, your heavenly Father will also forgive you: but if ye forgive not men their trespasses, neither will your Father forgive your trespasses" (Matthew 6:14-15).

If I were asked to pinpoint one thing that is required for healing above all else, it would be so difficult to answer. If pressed, though, I would have to say it is forgiveness. Healing and salvation ultimately rest upon our forgiving those who wound us. Many people will not be healed, even after reading this book, and the reason is their lack of forgiveness. The biggest hindrance to healing is an unforgiving spirit.

It is vital that we come to a better understanding of what forgiveness means. Our salvation can depend on it. The Bible tells us that no sin can enter into heaven. It also says, "If we say that we have not sinned, we make him a liar, and his word is not in us" (I John 1:10). The only way to get rid of our sin is to confess it to God so that He can forgive it. "If we confess our sins, he is faithful and just to forgive us our sins, and to cleanse us from all unright-eousness" (I John 1:9).

God will not turn away anyone who comes to Him in

repentance. He loves to forgive. It is His nature to forgive. God forgives all types of wrongdoing. Christ died for us while we were still ungodly, sinners, and His enemies (Romans 5:6, 8, 10).

Yet the Bible also teaches that if we refuse to forgive others, then God will not forgive us. Jesus said in Mark 11:25-26, "And when ye stand praying, forgive, if ye have ought against any: that your Father also which is in heaven may forgive you your trespasses. But if ye do not forgive, neither will your Father which is in heaven forgive your trespasses."

"But I Can't Forgive—Him!"

Yes, you can. You can forgive even him. God commands it, and He never commands anything without giving us the ability to obey.

The Lord Himself has given us a pattern to follow. He forgave perfectly and left us an example. "Even as Christ forgave you, so also do ye" (Colossians 3:13).

How did He forgive? Jesus cried out from the cross, "Forgive them!" Forgiveness cost His enemies nothing, but it cost Him His life. And it could very well cost us. But it will also free us!

We are to follow in His steps (I Peter 2:21). We are to be conformed to His image (Romans 8:29). When we are committed to this cause, we can rest in the promise of Romans 8:28 that all things will work together for our good.

Forgiveness does not mean we justify a wrong, ignore it, or treat it lightly. We recognize that what was done to us was very wrong, but then we choose to blot it out. We choose not to remember it. We choose not to hate the wrongdoer but to pray until we overcome our bitter feelings against him. Isaiah 43:25 says that God blots out our sins for His own sake. "I, even I, am he that blotteth out thy transgressions for mine own sake, and will not remember thy sins." Let us blot out the sins of others, for His sake.

Psalm 103:12 tells us, "As far as the east is from the west, so far hath he removed our transgressions from us." There is no "East Pole" or "West Pole," only a North Pole and a South Pole. In other words, there is no measurable distance between us and our sins; God removes them to an infinite distance from us.

"I Can Forgive—But Not Forget!"

This attitude is a real stumbling block. I hear this statement over and over. Many people stop right here, but true forgiveness includes forgetting. When God forgives us, He forgets our sins, and we must do the same with others.

What, exactly, does it mean to forget? Sometimes conscientious people, who are trying to obey God, feel that because they have not been able to wipe a memory away they have not forgiven. Is this true? Does forgiveness really mean that we will never again remember that a certain person abused us? No, for if that were the case, most of us would live under guilt and condemnation for the rest of our lives, for we cannot literally wipe away these memories from our brains.

Does forgiveness really mean that we will never again remember that a certain person abused us?

Forgiving and forgetting is a choice not to let the past influence us in the present. Paul said, "I count not myself to have apprehended: but this one thing I do, forgetting those things which are behind, and reaching forth unto those things which are before, I press toward the mark for the prize of the high calling of God in Christ Jesus" (Philippians 3:13-14). Paul did not mean that his memory was utterly wiped out, but he simply put hurtful things behind him and moved on. The key to forgiving and forgetting is to do what he did.

How was Paul able to do this? Philippians 4:4-9 gives us some good information in this regard: "Rejoice in the Lord alway: and again I say, Rejoice. Let your moderation be known unto all men. The Lord is at hand. Be careful for nothing; but in every thing by prayer and supplication with thanksgiving let your requests be made known unto God. And the peace of God, which passeth all understanding, shall keep your hearts and minds through Christ Jesus. Finally, brethren, whatsoever things are true, whatsoever things are honest, whatsoever things are just, whatsoever things are pure, whatsoever things are lovely, whatsoever things are of good report; if there be any virtue, and if there be any praise, think on these things. Those things, which ye have both learned, and received, and heard, and seen in me, do: and the God of peace shall be with you."

Paul learned through prayer and supplication with thanksgiving, to be anxious for nothing. Instead of worrying about problems, he took his hurt and grief to God and left it there. He gave the sins committed against him and the persons who had hurt him to the Lord, for He is the Judge. After doing this, he had the peace of God, which kept his heart and mind. Whenever hurt reared its head again, Paul continued to think on good things. In this way, Paul no longer had to hold anothers person's sin against him. He did not mention or bring it to mind again. He did not keep an account. In verse 9 he instructed us to do the same things he did.

We cannot, with just a swipe, make our minds a clean slate. We have to work at it, for we are not perfect yet. Paul spoke of not yet being perfect and of forgetting the past in the same breath (Philippians 3:12-13). We are to strive for perfection, and one way to do so is to learn to control our thoughts.

We can do nothing apart from Him. He can help us overcome our memories, and He has already cleared away many ugly memories from our minds! (We cannot remember how many!) The point is, He is in control. "Can the Ethiopian change his skin, or the leopard his spots? Then may ye also do good, that are accustomed to do evil" (Jeremiah 13:23). We cannot do good on our own. If we do anything good, it is because of Him! In John 15:5, Jesus tells us, "Without me ye can do nothing."

"Let us run with patience the race that is set before us" (Hebrews 12:1). Let us forget the things that are behind and run toward the prize. Let us keep on running with Jesus!

"I Can't Forgive God"

I hear this statement a lot, but nowhere in Scripture do we find that we are to forgive God for anything.

Some people blame God for the circumstances of life, and they find themselves in terrible straits because of it. Lily told me, "I'm sorry, but I cannot understand a God who would sit there and do nothing while I was being [assaulted]." She sat stiffly as I tried to lead her to a better way of seeing it. Her jaw was tight, her mind made up. "No good God would just stand by and do nothing and watch His child hurt like that. I'm sorry!"

I am sorry, too, but God is a good God. His way is perfect (Psalm 18:30). He is not to blame for the sin of the human race and the fallen state of the world in which we live. Martha had a wrong attitude, too, because Jesus came too late to suit her, and in the meantime her brother, Lazarus, died. The Scripture tells us how much He loved this family. Still, He tarried after learning that Lazarus was deathly ill. Put another way, He just "stood by and did nothing" while Lazarus breathed his last breath. At the time, however, no one knew of His plan to resurrect Lazarus.

Here was Sister Christy's attitude: "I had wanted the Holy Ghost and had been going to church. One morning my husband decided to go with me—and God filled him with the Holy Ghost with the evidence of speaking with other tongues! Now why did God do *that*? A spirit of anger and jealousy filled my heart, and I was angry with God. I'm better than he is, I thought. How could You do this to me? I immediately stopped attending that church."

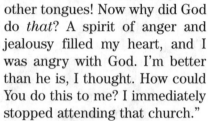

A spirit of anger and jealousy filled my heart, and I was angry with God.

We can get some strange notions in our heads. But God's way is perfect, and His plan and purpose for each life is also perfect. Lazarus suffered until he died. Sometimes we too must suffer. That is not God's fault.

To say that God needs to be forgiven is to imply that God has sinned. God cannot sin. To say that God must be forgiven is an affront to His perfect way, to His holiness, to His love for each of us.

And yet, if we hold such feelings in our hearts, they must be dealt with. We must be honest with God and tell Him how we feel. He already knows anyway. We have to let go of these feelings and put God back into His rightful place in our life.

God will not ask our forgiveness, for He can do no wrong. Nevertheless, God is so wonderful that He understands us, knows what we have experienced, and reaches out to us despite our wrong attitudes towards Him. He was waiting for Sister Christy all the time. He saw the things that went into making her the kind of person she was, one who would grow up to accuse Him. Christy explains:

"By the time I was fifteen years old, rejection—a lack of love and attention—filled my heart. I considered suicide, but God kept me even then. At sixteen, I was pregnant and had a son out of wedlock, looking for love in all the wrong places. My mother was enraged and would literally curse me out every day. She would say things like, 'You're just like your pa, a liar, a sneak, and you'll never amount to anything.'"

Sister Christy, like so many of us, went through many things that only she and God know about. The pain, the scars, the wounds—God knows them all. He understands, and He stands ready to forgive.

Being Reconciled

But I say unto you, that whosoever is angry with his brother without a cause shall be in danger of the judgment: and whosoever shall say to his brother, Raca, shall be in danger of the council: but whosoever shall say, Thou fool, shall be in danger of hell fire. Therefore if thou bring thy gift to the altar, and there rememberest that thy brother hath ought against thee; leave there thy gift before the altar, and go thy way: first be reconciled to thy brother, and then come and offer thy gift (Matthew 5:22-24).

James 4:17 says "He that knoweth to do good and doeth it not, to him it is sin." If we refuse to forgive, that would be to know to do good and not do it. If we have this sin in our lives, our prayers will be hindered. We cannot ask according to God's will if we deliberately withhold something from Him. We will remain in bondage. The hurt will continue to drain us spiritually.

If we continue in sin, such as by refusing to forgive, God will discipline us so that we will repent. (See Hebrews 12:5-11.) Perhaps that is why we continue to feel pain in some situations. Hebrews 12:1 tells us to lay aside the sin that so easily besets us. Could that sin be unforgiveness in our lives?

Sometimes people imagine that someone has done

something to offend them, even though the suspect is completely innocent. For example, Sister Mary got it in her head that I had betrayed a confidence of hers. Actually, she had already told several people about her problem (also in confidence), and her confession got around. Anyway, I sensed she was upset about something, but I had no idea what. According to Matthew 5:23, I felt she had "ought" against me. According to verse 24 I needed to go to her and seek reconciliation.

God takes such a matter very seriously, for verse 22 says we are in deep trouble if we are angry without a cause. The instruction to leave the altar before offering our gift to God in order to seek reconciliation also shows the seriousness of the matter.

So I went to my sister. "Have I done anything to offend you?"

"You betrayed my confidence."

I was innocent. Should I ask for forgiveness? I did not want to imply that I was guilty, for that was false, and we are not to lie. We do need to communicate, however; we need to talk over our problems so we can be reconciled with one another. In a case like this, we express our love and concern, and state our innocence. (If we are guilty of wrongdoing, of course we need to confess and ask for forgiveness.) We must do all we can do to be reconciled. Then we can return to the altar and complete the work we started there. The point is that it is vitally important to keep our hearts right.

Will God come to us if we have "ought" ("any kind of thing," according to *Strong's Concordance*) against Him? His Word instructs us, even when we are innocent, to go to our brother if he has something against us. It could well be that God has already come to us. He may have already worked through circumstances to bring us to the point where we change our attitude towards Him. There is no cause to be angry with God. We must make things right with Him. The person who blames God for his problems, however, sees these very circumstances as a reason to blame Him even more. "If God cared about me," he may say, "He wouldn't let this happen to me." In reality, because God loves us and does not want us to be lost, He may allow painful circumstances in our lives so that we will recognize our sin and turn to Him.

One definition of "forgive" in *Webster's Dictionary* is "to give up resentment against or the desire to punish; stop being angry with." In this sense, then, we may find ourselves having to "forgive" God; that is, we may need to give up a resentment against Him, to stop being angry with Him.

God also comes to us through His Word. As we go to God, we should pray that He will help us lay aside all resentment and anger. It is good to pray with the Bible in hand and allow God to wash us with His Word. As we read it and meditate on it, God will truly "explain Himself" through His Word. The more we come to understand God, the more our anger and resentment will melt away.

I have been so hurt and so angry at times that I did not feel I would ever be able to forgive. But one gentle word from the "offender" and I would melt. One time my pastor and his wife promised to be at the hospital for my surgery. The day came and went and they did not appear. I reasoned and made excuses for them, but after several days passed with no word, I gave in to the hurt. In self-pity I said to myself, "I was up there in that ole hospital all by myself; nobody was with poor li'l me; they didn't even come when they said they would," and so on, *ad nauseum*.

The next time the pastor's wife saw me, she instantly remembered. Dropping everything, she ran to my side, sobbing. "I'm sorry! I'm *so* sorry! I forgot all about it! Please forgive me, pleeeease!"

She looked so vulnerable, hunched over with huge

tears flowing without shame. How could I not forgive? All my hurt instantly vanished; it melted away totally. Our relationship was restored on the spot. My love and respect for her deepened because she had followed the Scriptures: "Go humble thyself and make sure thy friend" (Proverbs 6:3).

Salvation

Surely he hath borne our griefs, and carried our sorrows: yet we did esteem him stricken, smitten of God, and afflicted. "But he was wounded for our transgressions, he was bruised for our iniquities: the chastisement of our peace was upon him; and with his stripes we are healed. All we like sheep have gone astray; we have turned every one to his own way; and the LORD *hath laid on him the iniquity of us all. He was oppressed, and he was afflicted, yet he opened not his mouth: he is brought as a lamb to the slaughter, and as a sheep before her shearers is dumb, so he openeth not his mouth. He was taken from prison and from judgment: and who shall declare his generation? for he was cut off out of the land of the living: for the transgression of my people was he stricken. . . . He had done no violence, neither was any deceit in his mouth. . . . By his knowledge shall my righteous servant justify many; for he shall bear their iniquities. . . . He poured out his soul unto death (Isaiah 53:4-12).*

Jesus has already paid the price for our salvation. He has borne our grief. Long, long ago, He picked up all our sorrows and carried them upon His shoulders. He was stricken, smitten of God, and afflicted—for us. His work of salvation brings forgiveness to us and enables us to forgive others.

Salvation is a process that will continue until we have passed from this life. Salvation is not just a one-time deliverance from an ungodly lifestyle, but it is a continual process of healing and deliverance. I John 1:7 speaks of the continuous experience, relationship, and work of salvation in our lives: "If we walk in the light, as he is in the light, we have fellowship one with another, and the blood of Jesus Christ his Son cleanseth us from all sin."

We need the continuous work of salvation in our lives—salvation from fears in the night, loneliness, hopelessness, hurt, and pain. We need continual salvation from compulsions and addictions, from deadly and ungodly thoughts, from thoughts that can drag us into the depths of depression and discouragement. We need salvation yesterday, today, and tomorrow. Salvation includes the healing of hurts—hidden, secret, or just the usual day-to-day hurts. It includes being delivered from them and their effects on our heart.

When the hurting are told that they already have everything they need in Jesus, that is true. This statement does little for them, however, because they do not know how to appropriate the healing they need. They need to learn how to embrace the salvation they have received and appropriate it on a continual basis.

Receiving salvation on a continual basis means that it is working all the time, steady and without interruption. Nevertheless, from time to time we must call upon the Lord for salvation from a particular problem. Deliverance is available all the time, but we must grasp it and bring it into our own lives on a personal and practical basis. It is like a gift wrapped in beautiful paper with streaming ribbons and bows. We know we have the gift because we can see it sitting on the table, but it does us no good until we unwrap the package and begin to use what is inside. When we use the gift, we are appropriating it *continually*.

Jesus is our salvation. We sometimes get confused because one person tells us, "Use His name," while another tells us, "Use His blood," and someone else says, "Pray and fast." Yet another tells us, "Read the Bible," and another says, "Bind the spirit." We obediently try all these things, and still we are not healed. All of these suggestions have merit, but we must recognize that they all express ways of focusing on Jesus and His saving work. Through prayer, church attendance, and study of the Bible, we can develop a relationship with Jesus, the living Word, and appropriate His work of salvation on a daily basis.

A Personal Word in Your Pain

You cry out: "But . . . the LORD hath forsaken me, and my Lord hath forgotten me!" (Isaiah 49:14). Our Lord tenderly answers in verses 15 and 16: "Can a woman forget her sucking child, that she should not have compassion on the son of her womb? Yea, they may forget, yet will I not forget thee. Behold, I have graven thee upon the palms of my hands; thy walls are continually before me."

When you find yourself alone, remember your Lord. He always is there. When everyone else has given up on you, when you have called for prayer and no one is home, you have His word that He is there for you.

God uses people to repair people. We are His hands, His feet. God, all by Himself, can do it. God came to me in the darkest night of my soul. He brushed my cheek with His holy kiss and whispered to me from the shimmering leaves of an overhead branch. It is God's love that wins the sinner, not His judgment. God's love is pure and holy, but it is also the most powerful force on the face of the earth. That is why we must yield, so that this love can flow through us to other hurting people.

In conclusion, let me share what I believe the Lord is telling hurting people in the church today:

"The day is coming, My child, when you will run to and fro upon the face of the earth and can find no one to help, no one to pray. You must be able to stand. You must be able to see Me and hear Me and allow Me to be your strength. Now is the time, my child, to get to that place. Now, while you are surrounded by people of God, by people who love you and who care, even though they might not understand. Let Me be your God, let Me love you, let Me be your ever-present help in time of need and struggle. I love you with an everlasting love, and it is My will that you be whole and that you be strong. It is My will that you reach out to the lost and wounded and that you be a channel through which I can bring them unto Me. If you won't do it, My child, who will? If you won't reach out, who will? There are souls that only you can reach, that only you can communicate with, that only you can draw to Me with My love through you. Love Me, my daughter, as I love you from the beginning of time."

Chapter 22

A Final Word to the Christian Leader

"Jesus saith to Simon Peter, Simon, son of Jonas, lovest thou me? . . . Feed my sheep" (John 21:17).

Jesus asked Peter this question three times. He told Peter to feed His lambs, and then He told him to feed His sheep. Peter had failed God terribly—He had denied our Lord. Yet Jesus still loved him, still worked with him, and still planned to use him. How awesome is our Lord!

It is my prayer that something in this book will help leaders minister to the hurting. For years it has been my dream to see every church have a biblical counseling department or counselor. Even if a church has only one person, he or she should be trained in how to counsel the children of God biblically.

I was trained in traditional, clinical psychology. I received university training and was employed in secular environments. My ideas are based on my experience as both a secular counselor and a biblical counselor. I have seen both sides. There is an old expression: "Don't throw the baby out with the bath water." We should be careful not to throw out all the insights from the field of professional counseling simply because some things in it are bad.

As we have seen in the preceding chapters, new converts today bring problems with them that many of us have never even heard of. I have had to work with things that I could not even mention in these pages. It is a rare person who receives the Holy Ghost and never again has a problem with his or her past. Receiving the Holy Ghost is the beginning, not the end. Too often, we look upon the new-birth experience as the end of the story, but it is not the end. For many people, there is much suffering yet to come and much feeling alone in that suffering. We are supposed to feed these lambs, but how?

What about people who have been in church long enough to grow into sheep? We are supposed to feed them also. Are we aware of the needs of the people who sit in our pews? Do we know what really hides behind those sweet Holy Ghost smiles? I am working with three clients, for example, all of who have had the Holy Ghost for over fifteen years, and all have backgrounds of Satanic ritual abuse. One lady told me, "I'm just not sure that the blood of Jesus really applies to me because I was sacrificed to Satan, with blood, when I was five years old."

I know the poignant loneliness that results from the false belief that I am the only one who is suffering so greatly.

Our precious people can have strange ideas in their heads because of their past. I know very well that there are many hurting people filling our churches. I know personally what it is like to sit on the pew, service after service, month after month, hurting inside, looking around at everyone else, and seeing no one else who seemed to be hurting. We can be lonely in the middle of a crowd!

All the pretty Pentecostal ladies with not an uncut hair out of place can seem intimidating to those who already feel inferior. (Of course, the Bible teaches ladies not to cut their hair, and there is no prettier sight on earth than a Pentecostal lady!) I know the poignant loneliness that results from the false belief that I am the only one who is suffering so greatly. I used to look at the ladies who seemed so perfect. I was absolutely certain—but wrong— in thinking that none of them had struggled with the ugly things I had.

Since not every church has someone who has been trained in counseling biblically, there may come situations where there is no one to help. Great damage can result when we try to counsel someone who has a problem total- ly beyond our level of training and experience. What is a pastor or other leader to do when a saint desperately needs counseling that no one is trained to give? It is time to refer the person to someone who can help.

Some words of caution are in order, however. Just because someone calls himself a Christian counselor or a Christian psychologist does not mean that is what he real- ly is. Many call themselves Christian who do not meet the biblical definition of the word, and some do not even rely on the Bible as the final authority in counseling. Some so- called Christian counselors have advised our people not to go to church so much and not to be so "radical" in their spiritual beliefs. I have known precious sheep who have gone to a counselor such as this and eventually left the church.

A true biblical counselor will have as a goal the devel- opment of people spiritually. He or she will help them find a closer walk with Jesus Christ, knowing that spiritual growth is the ultimate solution for all problems. Such a counselor will understand that healing is not just learning how to cope, but true healing is being set free to serve God to the fullest.

Today "Christian" psychology is big business. Many people—even worldly people—have been wounded so badly by secular counselors that they are seeking something different and something better. Even for those who do not know what genuine Christianity is, the word "Christian" implies a certain kind of wisdom and compassion that they do not find anywhere else. As a result, people have been turning to Christian counselors by the droves. Adding some Bible verses to one's psychotherapy can become quite profitable.

Therefore, we must take care when we refer a child of God to counselors, even if they claim to offer Christian counseling. We need to find out if they live a moral life and if they truly base their counseling on the Word of God. For instance, would we want someone who lives in fornication, homosexuality, or drunkenness to advise and counsel our own children? Or would we want them to obtain counsel from someone who seems to live a moral life but does not promote life choices that are in accordance with the Word of God?

I am personally acquainted with a well-known Christian psychologist. He is an upright, moral man with strong family values, but he has absolutely no insight into the Apostolic way of doing things. He also believes it is acceptable to add psychology to Scripture and vice versa. The Word of God, however, says we must neither add to it nor subtract from it. "Ye shall not add unto the word which I command you, neither shall ye diminish ought from it, that ye may keep the commandments of the LORD your God which I command you" (Deuteronomy 4:2). "Add thou not unto his words, lest he reprove thee, and thou be found a liar" (Proverbs 30:6). II Peter 3:16-17 further warns us not to be like the "unlearned and unstable" who "wrest . . . the . . . scriptures, unto their own destruction."

We cannot afford to mishandle the Word of God.

God's Word contains everything we need for a whole and fulfilled life.

As a biblical counselor, my own walk with God must be genuine and growing. The Lord has to be first in my life in order for me to help anyone else. As I put Jesus first, my faith in His sufficiency blossoms and grows. I help my clients when I stress that Jesus is all in all. I must lead them to Jesus, for He is all sufficient. He can be all things to all people. He is the answer to every problem. He is the healer.

We must minister healing to hurting people! We must pour oil on their wounds and break bread for them. We cannot let them die! God loves them, and He has a job that only they can do. Let us strive to become biblical counselors and minister to them in love. Jesus said, "By this shall all men know that ye are my disciples, if ye have love one to another" (John 13:34).

As I sat in a restaurant one day, trying to calm myself between pressing and important appointments, I found myself thinking impatient, ugly thoughts about the people in the next booth. Not only were they polluting the place with cigarette smoke, they were also loud and obnoxious, and they utterly destroyed the tranquillity that I felt I needed at the time. I sent what might have been some unholy looks their way.

The Lord gently chided me, reminding me of my redemption and of their lost condition. I said, "Truth, Lord. But there's no excuse for their behaving that way. Look at them! Move on them, and make them stop."

The Lord responded, "No, *you* stop. Grow up. Pray for them as I have taught you. Don't you know how much I love them and need you to inquire of Me for them? I have given you a ministry of intercession. That is a ministry to be used anywhere at any time. See that woman in blue? You don't know her but I do. She's a backslider. I want her back. Pray, child, pray!"

I am ashamed that the Lord had to deal with me that way. My selfishness shames me! I am thankful for a God who knows us and who continues to love us, train us, and lead us gently.

So much of the time we have our own agenda. We think we know how things are supposed to go and how they should be done. For example, we may become impatient in listening to a person's problems. Sometimes I am so busy that my mind is racing along on many other paths, and there stands before me someone with a problem. I listen with half a heart sometimes, but I am striving to improve, because each person deserves my respect. If I agree to listen to someone, then I should do her the courtesy of *listening*.

Here are some general guidelines for working with hurting people.

1. *Listen to them*. Do not cut them off. Do not race ahead to what you think they might be going to say—or to what you think you want to say. Do not formulate your answers or advice, or prepare pat scriptural statements as they talk. Really listen.

2. *Do not appear shocked by anything you hear*. Such a reaction can frighten the victim into going back into silence.

3. *Be empathetic, not merely sympathetic*.

4. *Be supportive, but do not support any weaknesses*. For example: "I understand how you might feel that way, Sister Smith, but to continue drinking will destroy you. Let's look at some things that might help."

5. *Lead the people out of denial and into confession*. For example, consider a rape victim who is innocent of wrong and is not responsible for the attack in any form or manner. Still, as a result of the rape, there may now be some sin in her thought life that must be confessed and repented of. Does she hate her attacker? Is she able to truthfully and from her heart? Can she forgive him? If she

harbors sinful attitudes, they belong to her and she must deal with them. We must train people to confess sin, repent of it, and accept God's forgiveness. Then we should speak words of faith to the freshly cleansed heart.

6. *Help people focus not on the problem but upon Jesus, the problem solver.* Some people talk more about their symptoms than about God's ability and desire to heal. We must train people not to deny that there is a problem but to confess that God is *bigger* than the problem. He is bigger than *any* situation. He is the answer. He will work things out.

> *We must train people not to deny that there is a problem but to confess that God is bigger than the problem.*

Focusing on Jesus instead of the problem is not easy, but it works. It brings healing to a soul when possibly everything else has failed. We must focus on God and talk about God.

We must adopt the attitude of the Shunammite woman after her son, who had been given by God, died. She journeyed to Elisha, the man of God, and he sent his servant to greet her. "Run now, I pray thee [said Elisha] to meet her, and say unto her, Is it well with thee? Is it well with thy husband? Is it well with the child? And she answered, It is well" (II Kings 4:26). Despite the circumstances, we, too, must say, "It is well"—when the police department calls because our child is down there . . . when the highway patrol knocks on the door . . . when our spouse goes into the operating room alive and does not return that way . . . when our world falls apart all around us. "Faith is the substance of things hoped for, the evidence of things not seen" (Hebrews 11:1).

When we turn our eyes to Jesus and off our pain, He is able to do something about the pain. We must stop believing merely in "facts," for Jesus is the fact changer! The doctor may say the *fact* is that the cancer is inoperable. Maybe that is so. But Jesus changes facts!

Once a person had a tumor, but after prayer there was none. The doctor had the patient sign a release of liability. He was afraid of legal action, because he knew there had been a tumor and had told the patient about it, but then it was gone. He did not know what happened to it.

But we do!

Bibliography

Adams, Jay. *Christian Counselor's Manual.* Grand Rapids: Zondervan. 1973.

Allison, Lynda. *Lord, Why Am I Crying?* Los Angeles: By the author. 1992.

Augsburger, David W. *The Freedom of Forgiveness.* Chicago: Moody Press. 1988.

Cook, William H. *Success, Motivation, and the Scriptures.* Nashville: Broadman Press. 1974.

Foster, Timothy. *Called to Counsel.* Nashville: Oliver-Nelson. 1986.

Helminiak, Daniel A. *What the Bible Really Says about Homosexuality.* San Francisco: Alamo Square Press. 1994. Not recommended for a scriptural study.

Lovett, C. S. *Unequally Yoked Wives.* Baldwin Park, Ca.: Personal Christianity Publishers. 1968.

About the Author

Author of *Lisa Said No* • *Larissa's Song* • *Goodbye, Granny Dix* • *Lord, Why Am I Crying?*

DR. LYNDA ALLISON DOTY earned undergraduate degrees in journalism and psychology and master's and doctor's degrees in counseling. She received her Ph.D. in 1992. Her area of specialization is biblical and pastoral counseling. After twenty-four years of living single, she married again in 1997 to a minister who shares her burden for the hurting. She and her husband presently labor in Nebraska and South Dakota. Sister Doty is director of pastoral care in her local church. She also directs A Woman's Place, a healing ministry to "help women become all that God would have them to be," by learning to examine themselves according to the Word of God and then working on those areas that do not measure up.

Sister Doty evangelizes and conducts groups, seminars, and classes nationwide, teaching others how to apply the concepts of biblical counseling both in their own lives and the lives of others. She often spends several days at a church, ministering to the congregation as a whole and then having individual sessions with ladies referred by the pastor.

After you read this book, Sister Doty would love to hear from you. You may contact her at:

P.O. Box 1222

Bellevue, NE 68005-1222

E-mail: Hosanna@apostolic.net or Awomansplace@juno.com

Web site: http.//www.apostolic.net/awomansplace